In the Footsteps of Greatness

Josh Mathe

Library of Congress Control Number: 2014939864
ISBN: 978-0-692-23027-5
In the Footsteps of Greatness Softcover Edition 2014
Printed in the United States of America

For more information about special discounts for bulk purchases, please contact 3L Publishing at 916.300.8012 or log onto our website at www.3LPublishing.com.

Book design by Erin Pace-Molina

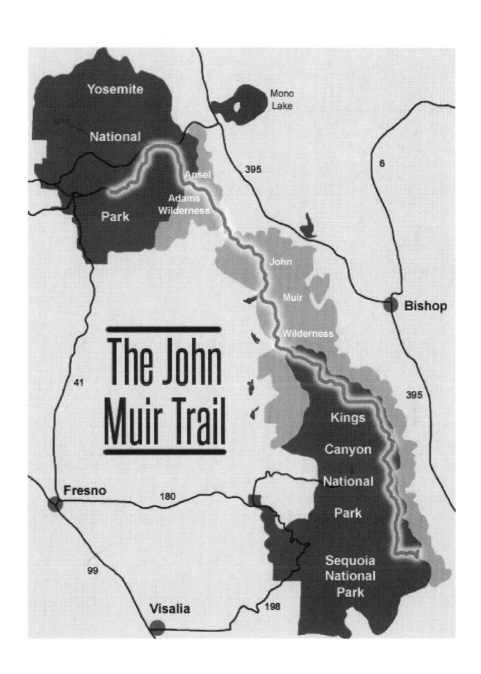

For my parents, who instilled in me a deep belief that all things are possible. And for those who love me and continue to show me that even though I want to be more, being me is enough.

Table of Contents

"It is not the critic who counts; not the man who points out how the strong man stumbles, or where the doer of deeds could have done them better. The credit belongs to the man who is actually in the arena, whose face is marred by dust and sweat and blood; who strives valiantly; who errs, who comes short again and again, because there is no effort without error and shortcoming; but who does actually strive to do the deeds; who knows great enthusiasms, the great devotions; who spends himself in a worthy cause; who at the best knows in the end the triumph of high achievement, and who at the worst, if he fails, at least fails while daring greatly, so that his place shall never be with those cold and timid souls who neither know victory nor defeat."

— *Teddy Roosevelt*

Introduction

"Each man's life represents a road toward himself..."
– Hermann Hesse

I suppose this story should start where any good story does — the beginning. I first laced up my hiking boots at the tender age of seven, and looking back it's amazing my dad had the audacity to suggest it and that my mom actually acquiesced given her penchant for safety and common sense. Regardless of the serendipitous circumstances that got me there, that first trip in a very real way set the tone for the rest of my life: my belief in myself and my athletic ability; the deep peace and connection I feel when surrounded by streams and forests; the smoldering fire that pushes me to test my limits and to find new challenges against which to throw my will and spirit. And perhaps most of all, the beginnings of a question that I've been compelled to answer again and again: Do I have what it takes?

I only have fleeting memories of this first backpacking trip. Twelve grueling miles in from Lake Victoria (Mammoth, CA), up over Duck Pass, and down into the secluded and verdant Cascade Valley. I remember being awed by my dad's Herculean strength, Eagle Scout skills, and lean, muscular physique — and desperately wanting to be like him someday. I remember catching trout by the dozens, using ladybugs as bait, and cooking them in garlic and wild onions. I remember being horrified and fascinated as my uncle's best friend regaled us with stories of his sexual escapades and being proud that I was considered man enough to be included. I remember drinking coffee for the first time and wondering why anyone would voluntarily consume it as I choked down its scalding bitterness. Ghost stories, crazy chipmunks, dreams of Quarter Pounders with fries, and one lost retainer — it's funny what I remember.

Yet there are things I don't remember like altitude sickness or my dad taking my pack and strapping it onto his because it was too much for me to handle. I don't remember being homesick or tired, the blisters or the hunger. It's funny what I remember, but also fascinating what I don't. Particularly because it is the pain that shapes us. Perhaps because it is so visceral and poignant you must look at it sideways like the sun. So even though I don't have a conscious memory of the challenges I faced on this trip so long ago on some deep level these experiences began forging me into the man I am today — both in my need to push myself as well as to explore the boundaries I find along the way.

But let's go all the way back to the beginning …

I grew up in Los Angeles (LA), and while the glamour and bustle may appear sexy through mature eyes, as a child it was terrifying. I was always on edge, and the only places I felt safe and confident were at home or on the baseball field. I stuck to my comfort zones and excelled, especially when everything went my way. But when it didn't? I would scream at my coach (my dad) as he walked out to comfort me on the pitching mound and cry the one or two times during the season that I struck out. Needing to be good and secure at this one thing in life, coupled with the yearning for my dad's approval was just too much for me to cope with in failure. It became so unmanageable that eventually an assistant coach was assigned to handle me. There were other scattered instances similar to these during those formative LA days, but this is a representative amalgamation of who and where I was at the time. I stayed mostly within myself, without really knowing myself, and had yet to gain any perspective or the tools necessary to deal with life's difficulties.

Then, in 1992 the Rodney King riots ignited our city. I remember sitting in disbelief in my Sherman Oaks classroom, watching the riots live on television, and wondering how people could act like that; wondering if it was even real; wondering if my dad would be safe. He worked in Englewood at the time, which was right in the heart of the destruction. Years later he would tell me and my sister the fateful circumstances of that day. How (just blocks from his office) four men descended upon a truck stopped in front of him at a stoplight. They dragged the driver from his vehicle, beat him to what appeared to be death, and firebombed the truck with Molotov cocktails. And then they turned to face my dad with wild hatred in their eyes. Filled with adrenaline he floored the gas, swerved around the carnage in front of him, and sped through the red light to safety. That night he and my mom decided to move the family out of LA.

This move happened to be fantastic for me. Perhaps I was just maturing, but if LA was the ideal crucible for toiling my earth and planting seeds, Northern California was the sunlight that allowed me to flourish and grow. I felt safe for the first time — externally, but also safe to be myself. Or to even explore whom "myself" was. And while I was beginning this process, my dad did some fundamental changing of his own. Up to that point he had been a fun and caring father, but he kept the rest of the world at arm's length. He was the guy who brought a book to parties so he wouldn't have to connect with anyone. And he had a large reservoir of hurt and anger that was usually just below the surface but would explode in hot geysers of emotion every now and then.

For some reason, his new boss in Northern California pushed all of his truculent buttons, and after months of ineffective communication he was given an ultimatum: do some personal growth or find a new job. So, he grudgingly signed up for a workshop that others in the company had attended, and it changed his life. I remember shortly after the workshop ended watching *Forrest Gump* with him and seeing him cry for the first time, and thinking "Whoa. Who are you and what have you done with my father?" But it was and continues to be an incredible blessing. He is warm, open, engaged, and connected — and perhaps like me, just needed the push and an opportunity to step into who he really was all along.

This program was so transformational and represented such a potent paradigm shift for my whole family that its effects were felt everywhere. The same company happened to offer a similar personal growth workshop for teenagers, and it quickly became an unspoken expectation that I would attend. In hindsight it's obvious that I was uncomfortable with this turn of events from the beginning, but at the time the waters were too murky to clearly see anything. I always did what my parents wanted of me, and it was exceedingly important to gain their approval and make them proud, so I agreed to attend the workshop.

It was awful. I experienced it as punitive, patronizing, and lacking authenticity. Most importantly I wasn't there for the right reasons. I was there for my parents and not for myself. Midway through the program, though, I came to this crashing realization and was instantly at peace. I still remember the crystal clarity and emotional quiet that enveloped me, as I knew in my bones what I had to do. What my real work was to be. So I quit. In the middle of an exercise I simply stopped and told the facilitator that this wasn't for me and that I was leaving. He went berserk. He got inches away from me, his face flushed and spittle flying everywhere, and screamed, "You are a quitter, and you will always be a quitter!"

And with those words ringing in my ears I walked out the door.

I know now he was just trying to motivate me. He didn't understand what I was going through or what I needed at the time. I harbor no hard feelings. In fact, that moment was pivotal for me. On the one hand I stepped into my own and "defied" my parents for the first time. This was powerful and confidence-building on a very foundational level. On the other hand, I did drop out of something I had committed to doing and heard the echo of the facilitator's last words bouncing around in my head. Was this true? Am I a quitter? Since then, I have been driven (sometimes obsessively) to answer this question.

Fast-forward to March 2003 and the end of a six-year relationship and eleven-month marriage. "We were just too young," she said. And she was probably right. I wrote off all the compromises and sacrifices as unavoidable and obligatory components of any long-term relationship (which may still be true), but the reality is that we just got caught in the momentum and never should have been together that long. Coming to the realization that it was over was like jumping into an ice-crusted river — numbing shock followed by a mixture of nausea and strange euphoria.

I was emotionally scattered for a while as I tried to rebuild the dream of what my life was to be. I went on a solo road trip for a few weeks. I visited my sister at UC Santa Barbara — and it was just me and all the girls in her dance major. Yeah. Not a safe place for a newly single and emotionally raw young man. Not surprisingly, I fell for one of her friends. Hard. Which was ridiculous but also wonderful because it once again helped me see the world in terms of possibilities and open doors.

As I healed and put the pieces of my life back together over the next few months, one of the possibilities that bubbled to the surface was the idea of hiking the entire John Muir Trail. Since that first backpacking trip, I had gone on many other outdoor adventures and the wild was in my blood. There was just enough danger, difficulty, and intrigue to get my juices flowing — and the more I thought about it, the harder it was to ignore. I especially liked the idea of taking my newfound freedom for a test drive. I had just quit my job and moved back home. (It was my first "real" job out of college. I was an auto underwriter for State Farm Insurance, and I assure you it was even less exciting than it sounds.) With no real ties or excuses, I decided to go for it.

Looking back, I can only smile at the naive exuberance of my 25-year-old self. I trained for a few weeks by loading a backpack with rocks and hiking up and down the American River Trail in Sacramento. I really had no idea how long it would take me or how many miles a day I would be able to cover, but I bought enough food for about two weeks. The trail technically runs some 212 miles from Yosemite Valley to the top of Mt. Whitney. However, I decided to hike the alternate route that starts below Mt. Whitney and go south to north. Setting out below Mt. Whitney because climbing to the top would be too hard? This decision is a perfect example of my mindset at the time. I wanted to explore; I liked the idea of testing myself; I enjoyed the attention for doing something unique; but I wasn't necessarily invested in earning it.

It poured rain the entire time I was out there, as if I was walking in God's garden and he was shadowing me with some vast watering can. Every square inch of my body and belongings were soaked. Hours of hiking in wet clothing and shoes does some interesting things to the body that I won't go into now because I have no wish to scar you for life. Suffice to say, I was incredibly uncomfortable. And the mosquitoes were relentless. Usually by early August the swarms have lessened, but a wet spring and mild summer had created the perfect conditions for optimal mosquito breeding. Plus my pack was heavy. And I was lonely. You get the picture.

Once the luster had worn off and the reality of hiking over 200 miles settled in, it was hard to remember why I was there. So, after a few days I invented some excuse that I could comfortably sink my teeth into (I don't even remember what it was ... probably bad chafing), and trudged 20 miles to the nearest trailhead. I arrived at dusk and was lucky to find a pair of hikers who were willing to drive me to a lodge a few miles away. Then I was blessed again as a family visiting from New York took pity on me. I can only imagine how forlorn and hapless I looked at the time. They bought me food, cheered me up, and let me sleep on the porch of their rented bungalow. The next morning my cousin picked me up and took me home.

I tried to convince myself that I had made the prudent decision. And I should commend myself for even attempting such a thing, right? I mean after all, most people just sit in cubicles all day, so I should give myself credit for living a life extraordinary ... shouldn't I? As good as I am at rationalization, some dark part of me knew better. I quit. I hadn't effectively prepared mentally, physically, or emotionally for an adventure of this magnitude, and when faced with adversity, I folded: John Muir Trail 1, Josh 0. Do I have what it takes? Not yet.

A couple years later the wandering spirit struck me again. This time I was in a relationship that wasn't going anywhere, and I had just quit another mind-numbing insurance job. Apparently having learned absolutely nothing from my last trip, I packed up my gear and went on a whim. I didn't even plan past the first couple days of the trip, just assuming I would figure it out as I went. This time I had decided to hike north to south, and my cousin (another one) dropped me off in Yosemite Valley. She actually hiked with me for a couple miles, and I have a strong sense memory of the deep loneliness I felt when she finally turned back and left me. I never recovered.

I hiked in a fog for the rest of the day, feeling every step of the monumental 5,000-foot climb out of the valley. When I met a father and daughter along the trail that night, I thought, "Why am I doing this alone?"

The next day I continued the negative self-talk disguised as wisdom. By that night I managed to convince myself that I had learned whatever I could from this trail, that my enjoyment of the natural world was mostly about experiencing it with people I love, and that I could return home fulfilled and self-actualized. I hiked out at Tuolumne Meadows (which would prove to be a little life foreshadowing) and waited most of the day for my thoroughly-annoyed girlfriend to come pick me up. This time I rationalized my decision even better, and only a minuscule part of me that I wouldn't even recognize until years later knew the truth — that I had quit again, and that my preparation had been even more abysmal than the first time: John Muir Trail 2, Josh 0. Not looking promising.

This brings us to the present. Since that second failed attempt roughly nine years ago, I am a different man in a completely different place. I have an incredible triathlon-goddess wife who loves me, challenges me, and inspires me. I have the lean lines of an endurance athlete, having become a decent triathlete and rather accomplished runner. I own a successful business that allows me to be immersed in my passion all day long. Life is exactly where I want it to be. Except that trail is still out there, whispering softly in my quiet moments:

"Do you have what it takes?"

I think I do this time … I hope I do.

Let's find out.

Authors note: In this book I refer to the total length of the John Muir Trail as both 212 and 223. The reason for this is that the trail technically ends at the top of Mt. Whitney (212 miles) but then one must still make it back to Whitney Portal and civilization (223 miles).

Also, I use "Mount Whitney" and "Mt. Whitney" interchangeably – simply two ways to identify the same enormous mountain.

Chapter 1
Training My Mind and Body

"By failing to prepare, you are preparing to fail."
— Benjamin Franklin

It was the fall of 2011 and I had just finished reading *Born to Run* by Christopher McDougall. We were celebrating our three-year anniversary at a quaint San Francisco hotel, and as I ran through Union Square on this oddly brisk Bay Area morning, I noticed that I was actually enjoying myself. For a former baseball player (and a husky one at that) turned average triathlete, that was curious and awesome. I smiled as I realized that I felt light and fast for perhaps the first time ever. Up to that point I had heard of the "runner's high," as if I were an explorer and it was some rare and elusive beast that was always one step ahead of me — about people who looked forward to running instead of simply bracing themselves for it and accepting it as an inevitable and uncomfortable part of staying in shape or completing a triathlon. But here I was cruising down the city streets like Prefontaine.

I'm not going to attribute my entire transformation to McDougall's book, but it did get me thinking about my run technique and opened me to the possibility that running could be fun. It also piqued my interest in trail running, which turned out to be a crucial piece of my story as an athlete. A little quicker turnover, a slight forward lean from my ankles, foot-strike more toward the ball of my foot. Add some belief and hope. Stir in a healthy dose of loping through the wild on dirt paths. Learn, improve, enjoy, repeat — this was the recipe that I just kind of stumbled upon and then actively engaged in as I felt its magic. And as I started sewing my running oats a bit, I looked with newborn eyes at the open world before me. What should I do with these fresh running chops?

The John Muir Trail whispers had been dormant for years as I had almost convinced myself that it was simply unattainable and unwise. Some things just aren't a good fit, right? However it was precisely this uncertainty that made some harder part of me want ... no, *need* ... to test myself again. Since the last JMT debacle I had built a business and completed an Ironman, so the mental barriers around my capabilities had been pushed back. I believed I could accomplish almost anything. It was the "almost" that decided it for me. I was going to return to the John Muir Trail. It would be hard - perhaps the hardest thing I'd ever done. But this time I would bring vastly more perspective, experience, determination, preparation, and humility. And I would stand on top of Mt. Whitney with my hands held high.

For this attempt I committed to cutting no corners and to investing myself completely in the experience. I would do absolutely everything in my power to prepare and to maximize my chances of success. I gave myself slightly less than a year to plan and train (I made the decision to go for it in the fall of 2012, and I would attempt the trail in August of 2013).

I then broke my preparation up into three phases:
- **Mental**
- **Physical**
- **Trip Logistics** (we'll get into logistics in chapter two)

I also upped the ante by announcing my intentions to anyone who would listen and by deciding to raise money for a fantastic organization called The Mission Continues. Whereas before I had kept my plans to myself and had given myself many outs, this time I left no room for failure. There is something scary but immensely powerful about speaking openly and plainly about your plans for success. The added pressure can be very uncomfortable, but it also sharpens focus and hardens resolve. It's much more difficult to quit when the world is watching you. Knowing this, I shouted my plans from the hilltops. And as I talked about success, I put in the roadwork that I thought would be necessary to make it happen.

MENTAL

This was huge for me, and in hindsight I believe it to be the difference-maker. I would love to say that I had it all figured out from the beginning, but that wouldn't be true. Forging my mind into the tool required to run 223 miles through some of the toughest backcountry terrain in the world was a wholly organic process, and it is only in looking back that I can describe the form and structure. It involved many pieces, some of which were inevitable outcomes of running long distances, and others that I consciously included because I had experienced their value in other aspects of my life. On a fundamental level, simply admitting and accepting that my mind would be the key to my success was a new and important step for me. And I knew that if I honed my skills enough, my brain could be a robust weapon when that trail challenged me. This was my JMT brain training:

GRATITUDE

There have been many books written about gratitude, and like most people I have heard self-help gurus expound on its virtues. I even started keeping a gratitude journal years ago, although I got bored with it after a couple days and moved on. But I had never made gratitude a conscious, daily practice. When I did, it instantly improved my running, marriage, business, and general outlook on life. There are countless ways to employ this tool, and I won't pretend to be an expert on the topic — I'll just tell you what worked for me.

Every morning, whether it's a 4:30 a.m. scramble to meet a client or the rare, casual awakening by the sun's first rays on my face, I take a moment. Before reaching for my phone to check email, before letting myself think of the countless tasks I have to complete that day, I stop and just "be". I breathe slowly, smile, and begin to think about what I am grateful for in that moment. It used to be virtually identical every day, like a memorized checklist, and when I realized that this lacked emotional firepower I decided to let each day's gratitude stand alone. I always make sure to sit with each aspect of my life that I am grateful for, just for a split second, and emotionally attach to it rather than just recite it dryly. If it's my mom I am grateful for, I see her in my head, hear her voice, and feel her smile. I feel how much we love each other, and let it hit me deeply. Then I move on. Sometimes it takes 10 seconds, and other times a few minutes. It is usually easy and fun, but sometimes I'm distracted and the best I can manage is a simple: "I am grateful to be alive." I always end with a smile and some version of: "I am grateful to be right here, right now, in this moment."

What this simple, daily practice does for me is profound. It sets my intention for the day. It helps me see the world as hopeful, connected, and passionate. It reminds me how lucky I am and insulates me from the little negativities that snipe at everyone all day. In terms of how gratitude helped me prepare for this JMT journey, I would say it set my mental stage. It cleared the chaff so that there was more room for courage and belief, helped me wake up every morning excited to run and to be in my body, and allowed me to feel enveloped by my fantastic network of support.

VISUALIZATION

Like gratitude, I employed the powers of visualization off and on, but never fully embraced its potency until I committed to this trip. It's funny how we often rebel against things we know to be extremely effective. Well, I won't speak for you — but I do. For instance, the night before Ironman Arizona I engaged in the most elaborate, lengthy visualization of my life. I saw each aspect of the day, from waking up to crossing the finish line, and mentally walked through all the minutiae in-between. Up to that point I hadn't given myself a time goal because it was my first Ironman and I just wanted to finish in one piece, but in that visualization I surprised myself by clearly seeing a time on the clock as I raised my arms and broke the tape. The next day the race eerily matched my imaginings, and I finished within seven seconds of the time I had seen in my head the night before. A race that takes over 12 hours, with so many factors you can't account for (like it taking me 10 minutes to put compression socks on after the swim because I couldn't feel my hands or feet), and I finished at basically the exact time I imagined? Are you kidding me? The implications of that power scared me quite frankly, and it took me until preparing for this adventure to fully step into it.

How I utilized visualization during JMT prep was twofold. First, I practiced focused visualization most nights before going to sleep. Second, I actively visualized during many of my longs runs. For both, the subjects of my visualization were very clear and defined: marriage, business, running. I would (and still do) start with one, see how I want things to be, and feel what that feels like. Then I open my eyes, smile, take a moment to come back to the present, and begin again with a different subject. Similar to gratitude, I've found that emotionally attaching to the visualization vastly increases efficacy.

This practice has, in a very tangible way, helped me create my reality and believe that I can. *Believe that I can*. That's an important phrase and central to this entire experience. I remember during a particularly good run sometime late last year stopping to text my wife, "I'm going to win a race next year." Part of me felt ridiculous. I had never been anywhere close to winning a race. But another part of me just knew it to be true. I started visualizing what it would be like to win a race. How it would feel to cross the finish line first, hearing the crowd cheering, and getting clapped on the back and congratulated by my competitors. I started thinking it was possible to hit faster and faster times on the track. During one time trial a friend of mine told me the time he'd gotten, and it seemed unattainably fast. But I couldn't let him beat me, so I tried to go that fast — and I did.

Then I won my first race, and since it was an out-and-back course I passed all the other runners on my way to victory. I distinctly remember the exhilaration of the wind on my face, lightly flying from root to stone, and then suddenly being aware that the other runners congratulating me sounded very familiar … because I heard their voices in my mind every night. The more I started exploring the power of belief, the more excited I became. I knew it could help me finally conquer that trail.

Specific to my JMT training, I saw myself enjoying every second of the trip, cresting each pass with a smile despite (and because of) the effort, and proudly planting my feet on top of Mount Whitney. I saw it and felt it till I knew it to be true.

POSITIVE SELF-TALK

For most of my adult life, I would have told you I was an exceedingly positive person. I think most people would describe me this way as well. And it would be true, up to a point. I realized however during long hours of running, that I had a bad habit of letting myself fall down rabbit holes of negativity. Most people have probably experienced this at some point, and the trigger can be anything: hunger, a tight calf, extreme heat, or even just coming into the run without mentally preparing for it. Regardless of the reason, I would latch onto it, wiggle it around like a loose tooth, and give it an increasing amount of focus and energy until I was in a dark mood and sick of running. As soon as I became mindful of this bad habit, I realized it was the prime de-railing mechanism of my previous JMT trips — and that I would actively need to address it during my training.

My strategy for overcoming this negative feedback was to identify and destroy. I did my best to stay mindful and be aware of the conversation I was having with myself at all times (not just while running). Then, when I heard my internal dialogue darkening, I would consciously replace that negativity with something uplifting.

A great example of this actually just occurred during a half-marathon I ran a few weeks ago. I was running 10-feet behind a good friend after I let him set the pace for the first few miles. This was by design as I knew he would try to bury me but that I could trust my endurance and pass him when he began to tire. All I had to do was keep up until then. Before the race I knew I could do it. For the first three miles I knew I could do it. Then all of a sudden I noticed how strong he looked, and how hard it was to keep pumping my legs so furiously. I wondered if I should just slow down now and find a more comfortable pace. Was he just too fast? A couple years ago that voice would have defeated me. This time I saw the rabbit hole coming, slipped in for a brief moment, and then said to myself: "You planned for this. You are right where you want to be. You have more speed endurance then he does and you understand the way he races. You are light and fast and can run like this all day. Stick with the plan, pass him when he gets tired, and you will run your fastest race ever." That's what I did.

I am by no means perfect at this exercise, and there are still times when I don't feel like running and can't claw my way out of the funk; but I became exponentially better at resisting negativity. The best part is that each time you are successful it builds new positive pathways in the brain, making it even easier the next time you are faced with a similar situation. The JMT implications of my new ability to identify and destroy negativity were monumental. A week alone in the backcountry facing extreme conditions would offer countless opportunities for negativity to creep in, and I had a feeling that this new arrow in my quiver would prove vital in making this trip outcome different than the others.

PHYSICAL

I am blessed that the best endurance-sport coach I know happens to sleep next to me every night. When I told my wife about my John Muir Trail intentions and asked her to coach me, she jumped on board with enthusiasm. Since she provided my training plan, I asked her to give an overview of what we did and why. She may not say it, and I know many people fail to see it, but great coaching isn't just about knowledge of the athlete and science — it requires a deep, artistic intuition as well. This gestalt is almost impossible to put into words, but hopefully this section gives a brief peek behind the curtain.

Jen:

It would be natural to assume that in order to prepare for a long event such as this the best prescription is simply to run a lot; however that approach is too simplistic. The reality is that we had to walk a strategic tightrope to continually push Josh's body (and brain) to a place of adaptation without under- or overdoing it — too little work could result in a lack of strength and endurance, and too much work would lead to injury and fatigue. Here's what we did:

Timeline

The John Muir Trail was the centerpiece for the entire year, however we really started to focus on it 4.5 months out from his first attempt. I gradually built up his weekly workload using non-linear periodization (a training philosophy where volume and intensity vary from session to session, as opposed to the more traditional linear periodization model where training is broken up into phases that keep the variables relatively constant within each phase).

Frequency

Five days a week. While we wanted to be smart about it, on a very basic level Josh's legs just needed to get used to running multiple days in a row.

Specificity

At least two workouts a week were trail runs, and often other easy runs would be on a trail as well when his schedule allowed. He also ran with a weighted pack during specific long runs. The more we could do to simulate the John Muir Trail experience, the greater his chances would be of success.

Recovery Time

Taking into account the impact of long runs, Josh ran no more than 2.5 hours at any one time, and the weekly training schedule was organized to allow for maximum recovery. Gradually as he became stronger, we adapted to active recovery (recovery using lighter exercise) between long runs; since he would need to run all day for a week while on the JMT, Josh would need to be able to recover on the run.

Volume

My philosophy is that every workout must have a specific purpose and that more is not necessarily better. As such, Josh's volume was lower than most would probably expect. His longest week was 12 hours, and that included a 50-mile race. Most weeks were five to seven hours, with a few weeks that built up to nine or 10 hours.

Speed Work

To keep volume lower (and recover quicker) we incorporated higher intensity training on a weekly basis. A weekly track workout, hill intervals, and intervals worked into longer runs. The idea was to increase training effect without increasing recovery time. Shorter quicker workouts can be recovered from in a few days, rather than long death marches that take a week or more to heal from.

Training Runs

We included planned races or events to allow the opportunity to practice fueling, carrying weight, overnight recovery, gear logistics, etc.

For the most part my physical preparation went fantastically. I was energetic and engaged, and because recovery and variety were maximized, I enjoyed myself and looked forward to virtually every run. And like anything else, once I started to see the results of my efforts it created a positive feedback loop, and I became even more motivated to put in the work.

My training was not without hiccups however. A couple months before I would attempt the John Muir Trail I drove down to the hills of San Jose, California to compete in my first-ever 50-mile race. Not wanting to break the bank (and apparently not having yet accepted the fact that I'm an adult) I booked a room at a quasi-hostel in a seedy little suburb a few miles from the race start. My poor judgment poked me when I discovered I would have to share a bathroom with the other guests, and then gave me a full kick in the groin when I wasn't able to sleep all night because of thin walls and arguing lovers.

Despite the inauspicious beginnings, I toed the starting line brimming with energy and belief. I felt like my body was prepared, and I was looking forward to the experience. When the gun went off I fell into a pace that felt sustainable, and even with that I quickly found myself cruising in second place. I began to flow, and before I knew it 20 miles had passed beneath my feet. But the trail was almost completely exposed, and the day had become increasingly warmer — and suddenly I could feel every climbing degree. It began to feel like my brain was on fire, and my decision-making ability and motor control plummeted. When I reached the aid station that marked the halfway point, I learned that everyone else had already quit or had been pulled off the course (other than the eventual winner who was a pro and performing well). The trail looped back on itself, and this aid station was also where the race started. I could see my car 50-feet away, beckoning me with its air conditioned comfort. I sat in the shade for 20 minutes, drinking Gatorade with ice and trying to ignore the constant string of earnest admonitions from the volunteers imploring me to stop before I hurt myself. I knew that 10 years ago I would have given up, and I think that's ultimately why I decided to keep going.

The next 15 miles were a hazy, stumbling blur. The only thing I remember clearly is the winner running past me on his way to victory, and how even he looked haggard. At some point I began laying down in the middle of the trail and daydreaming for a while before somehow dragging myself back up to move again. During one particularly long collapse, some functioning part of my brain pointed out that I was the only person out there, moving away from civilization, and that I might actually be in danger. When I allowed myself to see and accept that I was showing most of the early signs of heatstroke, I decided I had to turn back.

I slowly made it back to the start, walking and resting in every shady spot I could find along the way. As I will discuss a little later, I think there is a very fine line between quitting and being smart, and it takes maturity and practice to be able stay on the right side of that line. Could I have finished that race and survived? Maybe. I think I made the right decision however, particularly because the purpose was to train and learn for the John Muir Trail — which I did. I learned that I do better with less electrolyte supplementation, to avoid heavy exertion during the hottest part of the day if I could, and that running 50 miles in a row is ... hard.

A few weeks later, I ran the Double Dipsea. Beginning in Mill Valley and ending on Stinson Beach, the 7.5-mile Dipsea is one of the oldest foot races in the world and has been run every summer since 1905. Roughly twice as long, the Double Dipsea starts on Stinson Beach, reaches over Mt. Tamalpais to Mill Valley, and then returns to Stinson. Of all the places I've run this is perhaps my favorite, as every trail is painted with redwoods, beaches, and vistas that would be priceless if hanging in a gallery.

On this day, the Bay Area was unusually hot and my body had not fully recovered from the 41-mile meltdown. I had fun and did well, but the hills and heat took their toll. This was exacerbated by the fact that I was still attempting to dial-in the electrolyte situation and decided to eat and drink very little during the race (sometimes the dark side of being a nutritionist is that I know enough to experiment and get myself in trouble). After the race I guzzled water, but my body was already beginning to shut down — and I ended up in the hospital, hooked up to an IV, and thoroughly chagrined. (Jen loves this story because she had to make me call 911 even though I was on the side of the road too nauseas and dizzy to drive. Apparently I

Metabolic Efficiency

The other thing I did to maximize my endurance was to increase my body's ability to access and burn its own fat stores. The subject of fat adaptation can get very involved, and I don't want to focus too heavily on it, but it bears mentioning. We all have tens of thousands of stored fat calories in our bodies, and the more we can use those calories while exercising the less food we need and the more efficient we are. I knew this would be important since I would be moving all day long for multiple days in a row and simply would not be able to replace every calorie I burned — both because I couldn't carry that much food and because my body wouldn't be able to process it if I did.

The basic way I achieved this was to greatly increase my daily fat consumption, while decreasing carbohydrates (and eating carbohydrates strategically). It worked brilliantly, and I felt better when I was running and during my normal life. Blood and metabolic efficiency tests also revealed that my fasting blood sugar, systemic inflammation, cholesterol, and ability to burn fat at higher intensity levels all improved in just four weeks. In fact, science is starting to lean in this direction already, and there appear to be some very compelling reasons to adopt this dietary strategy for general health as well as sport performance. From a purely pragmatic perspective, I went from being an athlete who would become ravenous and weak after exercising for 30 minutes without food, to easily being able to run for up to three hours with only a water bottle and shoes (and perhaps a pair of shorts).

was trying to convince her over the phone that I wasn't dehydrated, although I have no memory of this detail.)

There were many other surprises in my otherwise perfect training season (including multiple poison oak outbreaks and a harrowing off-road adventure that almost destroyed my car), but I truly wouldn't have had it any other way; it is the blemishes that give the journey meaning and character and provide the contrast that make the highlights that much sweeter. And there were plenty of those too. Winning races, introducing my sister to the power of the trail, running free in some of the most spectacular parts of the world — even while I was walking it, I was grateful for every brick that lined my path to the JMT.

Chapter 2
Trip Logistics and Planning

"A goal without a plan is just a wish."
— Antoine de Saint-Exupery

Planning all the details and intricacies of an undertaking like this can be daunting, but I jumped into it with enthusiasm and ferocity. I recognized that simply flying by the seat of my pants as I had done previously was not an effective strategy. By nature I like to figure things out on the fly — both because details bore me and because I thrive on the energy created by pressure. But I have learned (particularly as a business owner) that there are certain things that simply work better if properly planned for. How I finally accepted this on a deep enough level to change my actions was to focus on the efficiency and success I could achieve with thorough preparation, rather than the process itself.

So I took out a piece of paper and brainstormed everything I would need to figure out.

- What direction would I hike?
- When would I go?
- How would I obtain a permit and how soon would I need to reserve it?
- How many days would it take me to complete the trail?
- What gear would I need to go as fast and light as possible?

- What shoes would I run in?
- How would I get to the trail and back?
- How much food would I need? Could I carry it all or would I need to resupply at some point along the trail?

Equipped with this checklist, the planning process was actually fairly painless and enjoyable. And every time I figured out another puzzle piece the dream became a little more tangible.

DIRECTION

I decided to start in Yosemite Valley and hike toward Mt. Whitney, trekking north to south. The merits of each direction are debatable, but I liked the idea of starting in one of the most beautiful valleys in the world and finishing on the highest point in the continental U.S. The downside is that the 11 passes I would have to traverse would be more difficult from my chosen direction, but I wasn't going for easy.

TIMING

In terms of timing, I have always liked August in the Sierras. Warm days, mild nights, and late enough in the season that snow and mosquitoes are rarely an issue. The only downside to August was that I had just qualified for the Olympic Distance Age Group National Championships (triathlon), and the race would be held August 10th. I sat with this fact for a few days, and eventually decided that I would completely forego triathlon is 2013 and commit myself entirely to preparing my body for this John Muir Trail run. Making this decision was difficult, but it was the right move. It allowed me to move forward with more focus, and I didn't regret it once. Calendar and conscience cleared, I took a deep breath and set my JMT start date: Monday, August 8th.

PERMIT

Permits can be tough to obtain, particularly in highly traveled areas, so I was encouraged when my research showed that I could reserve a permit that would cover the whole trail, and that I could it pick up in Yosemite Valley the day before my trip (I actually put a reminder in my phone for the first day I could reserve the permit, lost the reminder when I switched phones, and had to hope for a walk-up permit when I began my trip).

TRIP LENGTH

In deciding how long it would take to complete the trail, I wish I could give you some scientific extrapolation. In actuality it was an arbitrary number based loosely on how many miles per day I thought I could cover and not hike at night (so I wouldn't miss the scenery). Quite honestly I also wanted to do something a little extraordinary. Plenty of people have hiked this trail in two to four weeks. I wanted to run it. Target trail days — six.

GEAR SELECTION

The amount and type of gear to bring could be a book on its own, and I often found myself getting lost in the research for hours. There are so many options now for lightweight gear that eventually I just had to make some decisions and do my best. I chose to go absolutely as light and minimal as possible and to forego virtually all luxury items. I didn't even bring a toothbrush. I basically carried clothing, food, shelter, sleeping gear, water, and a couple other essentials. A few items of note that separated me as a "fast packer" vs. traditional backpacker:

- Tarp tent (tarp with mosquito netting sewn in), 11 oz
- Small, frameless pack, 1 lb 3 oz
- Down quilt (instead of sleeping bag), 19 oz
- SteriPen (UV water purifier), 3.6 oz
- No stove or cooking gear

*My entire gear list is included in the appendix at the back of the book.

SHOE SELECTION

Determining the best shoe for a journey like this deserved its own bullet point and attention. These constructed pieces of fabric and rubber would be the only thing between my feet and 223 miles of jagged High Sierra earth. They would have to be comfortable, light, durable, breathable, and fit my feet with just enough snugness to support but not constrain. It proved to be surprisingly difficult to find the perfect pair, and I went through six or seven different styles that I took on various training runs and races.

The **Brooks Pure Grit** were roomy, but didn't feel quite right.

The **Adidas Adipure Zero** were awesome road-racing shoes, but not made for trail running and quickly broke down.

The **Salomon S-Lab Sense** were beautiful (in fact I almost took them on the trip simply because of their high degree of badass-ness) and snug, but after 20 or 30 miles felt restrictive and gave me blisters.

I ended up choosing the **New Balance Minimus Trail 110** because they were light, comfortable, and just made me feel fast.

THERE AND BACK AGAIN

Getting to the trail and back wasn't going to be easy no matter how I organized it. Whitney Portal is on the east side of the Sierras and a solid six hours from Sacramento. Yosemite is four hours away and on the west side. I chose to caravan to Whitney Portal with my wife, drop my car, and then have her take me to Yosemite Valley to begin. I figured it would be easiest to not have to coordinate someone picking me up at the end of my trip and would allow me some wiggle room if it took more or less time to finish than I had planned on. It turns out this plan would change, but that's a story for a later chapter.

FOOD

In terms of what and how much food to bring, I chose to go simple. I didn't want to have to deal with cooking utensils or a stove, so I brought bars, meal replacement shakes, and one packet of smoked salmon per day (the fat, protein, and salt of the salmon turned out to be ideal, and I craved it all day long). Being a nutritionist, I created a detailed spreadsheet and shot for about 4,000 calories per day with a fat percentage as high as I could get it (turned out to be 51 percent of my daily calories). Even though storing your food in bear canisters is required for much of the trail, I made the conscious decision not to bring one because:

1) I didn't want to carry the weight.
2) I didn't want to use a pack big enough to fit a bear can.
3) I thought my baseball player arm could throw a rope to a high enough branch that my food would be safe from bears.

As you will soon discover, the decision not to bring a bear canister would greatly impact my trip.

*Detailed daily food list also included in the appendix.

RESUPPLY

There are a couple places along the John Muir Trail that help hikers resupply. You can put food, extra batteries, another pair of shoes, etc. in a painters bucket, seal it in a straight jacket of packing tape, write your name all over it, and send it to them. Then, weeks later, you roll in after a dusty day on the trail and pick up your goods (it's seriously cool, and much better than carrying more gear than you need to). I chose to go with one resupply that I planned to pick up at the Muir Trail Ranch, three days and 106 miles into my trip.

Training, planning, and preparation complete, I was now ready to head back to the wild — but I was not the same man who sulked off the trail all those years before. This time I was 15 pounds lighter and had spent years remaking my body in the forge of endurance sport. This time I had a sharper mind and tougher spirit. This time the trail would be mine.

Chapter 3
And So It Begins

"The mountains are calling and I must go."
— John Muir

As July wound down, I found my heart beating a little faster. I wasn't nervous per se, but I was chomping at the bit to smell the pine on the crisp alpine air and feel the twigs crack beneath my feet. It was very similar to the feeling I would get before a big game or standing in the corral a couple minutes before the gun went off at a triathlon. Alternating parts of my mind wanted to dig a hole and hide, cry (with both fear and elation), and laugh and whoop with enthusiasm. I mostly just yearned to stop thinking about the moment and be living in it.

Working through this anticipation was a great exercise in focus and compartmentalization, because I still had to work with clients, a wife to love, and the rest of my life to lead. I did fairly well during this period, however there was definitely a gradual sharpening of focus, as if I was a sniper looking down on the plateau that was my life — and then at some point I hunkered down, put the scope to my eye, and locked in on my target, the John Muir Trail.

And then suddenly it was Friday August 5th, and my excitement was finally assuaged. I accepted the well wishes of my last client, and as I headed home I finally let myself step completely into the experience. All the anticipation that had been trying to tear at my seams, and now it was beginning.

I had packed the night before, so all I had to do was quickly change clothes and grab my gear. I said a brief goodbye to the animals (we have a funny little Chug — a pug-chihuahua mix — and two cats that I have a mutual Cold War agreement with), and gave Jen a kiss as we each got into our separate cars. The plan was to drive most of the way to Whitney Portal that night and then find a hotel room when we couldn't stay awake any longer. Early the next morning I would leave my car at Whitney Portal, and then ride with her to Yosemite Valley — at which point I would try to get my permit and set up camp for the night, and Jen would continue home to Sacramento to hopefully get a long bike ride in (the need to plan everything around big workouts is a major hazard of the endurance athlete lifestyle).

Somehow we would need to get to other side of the Sierras and the easiest route is CA-89 toward Markleeville, and eventually 395 south down the eastern spine of the mountain range. We made great time for the first couple hours as we steadily climbed out of the foothills up Highway 50 toward South Lake Tahoe. As we turned onto the less-traveled 89, I immediately noticed the darkness. It was just us, four measly headlights, and a vast blackness. Both of us instinctively slowed down and stared at the road with increased vigilance. It was not uncommon for bears or deer to run in front of cars, particularly on this wild section of highway.

All night I had been trying to ignore a growing sense of unease, and unfortunately this proved to be prophetic. A few miles onto 89 we came around a bend to find the remnants of a recent landslide lying in the road. Jen was in front and had a split-second to choose:

- swerve left into the darkness on a very narrow mountain road;
- swerve right into the jutting hillside; or
- stay the course and hope the SUV had enough clearance.

She chose the latter (and rightly so), and instantly she was struggling for control of the car. There were sparks and smoke everywhere, and an alarm started blaring. She managed to keep going for a hundred feet and pull over on a small shoulder that had appeared. Endorphins on overdrive, I jumped out of my car to make sure she was okay. It turns out her brand new CRV has surprisingly low ground clearance, and as she passed over the largest boulder it struck the bottom of her car and got wedged between the plate and the ground. This had popped her airbag and triggered her car alarm (as each shrill note smacked my brain I found myself cursing the nice lady in the finance department who had offered the custom alarm for only a couple bucks extra every month). The good news was that other than a small laceration on her left hand and some shell shock, she was fine. The bad news was that we were in the middle of nowhere, with an un-drivable car that wouldn't stop yelling at us — and I kind of had someplace to be.

I quickly decided to reduce my stress by focusing on how Jen would get home safely and then worrying about my trip after that point. We stood there in bewilderment already beginning to flinch from the sharp bite of the wind. Before we had managed to formulate any lucid plan of attack, two high beams pierced the night and a large shadow skidded to a stop a few feet away. Just as I was bracing myself against this new development, dazzling blue and red lights lit the Ford Explorer from above revealing a CHP logo. Thank god. Law enforcement has helped me a few times in my life, but I can honestly say I've never been happier to pay state tax than I was in that moment.

"What seems to be the problem?" boomed the burly, baby-faced officer.

We explained the situation, and he quickly got under the hood of the CRV. After fiddling with a couple different things, he eventually managed to disconnect the battery and the night was suddenly silent. He told us that we were welcome to leave the car there overnight as we tried to contact our insurance company and figure out our next steps. Then he nodded, tipped his cap (I guess people still do that), and drove off.

It was a great deal easier to explore our options without the alarm scattering our thoughts. We decided to drive back to South Lake Tahoe, stay the night, and return to the car in the morning with a tow truck and/or my dad. My parents were coincidentally staying in a cabin in Tahoe that weekend so we hoped once we got back within cell phone range that we could connect with them for lodging and aid come sunup.

We did manage to get my dad on the phone, and he gave us amusing directions that only people who didn't grow up with MapQuest can provide. We made our way to the cabin, and after hugs and some theatrical storytelling, crashed into adjoining twin bunk beds (I think I actually tried to snuggle for a few minutes until we both realized that was going to be a great way to get absolutely no sleep).

With the dawn came perspective, and as we discussed the situation it became clear that all was not lost. My dad offered to pick me up at Whitney Portal at the end of the week, which meant I could drive myself to Yosemite Valley that morning without missing any time. Yosemite was only a few hours away, so I lingered a little longer than was required. I told myself I wanted to make sure Jen was taken care of, and it was true, but another small part of me wanted to bask in the glow of my family, starkly aware that I was about to be utterly on my own for a week. I think this is the dark side of having such a close, supportive family — if you're not careful you can begin to rely on them too much.

We were able to figure out the car logistics and how to get Jen back to Sacramento. And then it was time for me to say goodbye. I embraced my parents, aunt, and uncle, staying as light and chipper as possible so as not to worry them (I know my mom in particular was very uncomfortable about this trip, but she tried to be supportive). Then everyone graciously found something else to look at as Jen and I came together for the last time. She surprised me with tears in her eyes. My wife is beautiful, graceful, and wild — like an Arabian mare running free through the grass. She sometimes chooses to match my stride, but she sets her own course. And she can be as hard as granite when she needs to be. So to see the softness in her eyes, and the acknowledgement that she would miss me and fear for me, was both touching and sobering. We kissed, exchanged murmured endearments, held eye contact for long enough to say what words never can, and then I was gone.

As I drove toward Yosemite I made a conscious effort to be purely in the moment: feel the love from my family; enjoy my wife showing me that she needs me; and touch the sweet melancholy that only presents itself at moments like these. And at the same time to embrace the mounting excitement and skittering that ran up my spine when I thought about the adventure and unknown that tomorrow would bring. I could tell already that my mindset was different than at any time before, and that I now had a brightly burning flame of peace and stillness, surrounded by fortified walls of belief and experience.

Some hours later I found myself immersed in the bustle of Yosemite Valley. It is a curious juxtaposition; the banal and unseemly aspects of the human condition that occur in any large melting pot of people, plastered against some of the most breathtaking natural wonders in

Mindset

Over the years I have garnered a reverence and respect for the integral role our attitudes and expecations have in shaping our entire experience of life. The aforementioned positive self talk, gratitude, and visualization all played a part in building my bullet-proof mindset (or at least bullet-resistant. I am far from perfect at this). On a very basic level, I wouldn't reach Whitney if I was "hoping" to be successful. And certainly not if I was leading with my fear of failure. I would be successful only when, and because, I "knew" it would happen. There are countless fables and books about this force (*The Law of Attraction, The Secret, and The Magic of Thinking Big* are three that you may have heard of), and it captures the imagination because the power is real and seems supernatural. I can't tell you whether it is God, some universal energy, or simply our molecules responding to our thoughts, but I know from personal experience that you can actively change your mind, and your mind can change your world.

Fun challenge for extra credit

Contact the most successful person you know or can get ahold of, and ask them to chat with you about this topic. I guarantee they will have much to say, and what they share could very well supercharge your life forever.

the world. If you've never been, picture the most beautiful landscape you've ever seen and then put Times Square on top of it.

Anyway, I finally managed to find a parking spot and made my way to the Wilderness Center to get my trip permit. There are only 12 walk-up permits allowed per day, so I knew this could be dicey.

Worst case I could come back the next day when another 12 would be opened up.

The young ranger at the counter was helping someone else, so I had to wait for a few minutes, my tension mounting. This was the final logistical hurdle, and I was still kicking myself for the snafu that made this last-minute scramble necessary. I just stood there, breathing deeply, trying to remind myself that the trip wouldn't go perfectly and my ability to adapt to that reality would be paramount.

After what seemed like an eternity the ranger finished with the other couple and nodded for me to come over.

"I'm fast-packing the John Muir Trail and would like to get a permit," I announced, with more bravado than I felt. Not only was I afraid that no permits would be available, I was also uncomfortable about the fib I might have to tell.

"Doing the whole thing, huh? Good for you. How long do you plan that taking you?" she asked, eyes narrowing with appraisal.

"Well, I'm hoping to do it in six days, but we'll see."

"Wow, that's fast! Are you an ultra-runner?" she asked, tone of voice indicating that she was just now considering taking me seriously.

"Yep. Should be fun. Can't wait to get out there," I said aloud. "Come on, come on … just give me my permit and let me be on my way," I thought.

"When were you hoping to start? Unfortunately we don't have any more permits available today, and it looks like we already have a good 20 people hoping for tomorrow's slots."

"Ouch! Deep breath," I reassured myself. "I was really hoping to leave today or tomorrow. Do I have any other options?"

"Looks like there is room in Little Yosemite Valley tomorrow night. You can leave here tomorrow morning, stay in Little Yosemite Valley tomorrow night, and then continue on with your trip. Does that work for you?"

I wasn't particularly interested in that. Little Yosemite was only a few miles up the trail which would basically mean I'd lose an entire day. Not only did I want to challenge myself and complete the trail as quickly as I could, but Jen and I would be leaving for Whistler, B.C. almost immediately upon my return (she would be competing in Ironman Canada). My other option was to wait till the day after that, which would also potentially put me up against my timeline. I decided to take the permit and figure it out later.

"Perfect, I'll take it."

"Great. What kind of bear canister do you have?" she asked, looking down at the paperwork she had begun filling out.

And there it was: Should I tell her that I was planning to go so fast that I'd be out of Yosemite by the time I made camp and therefore wouldn't legally need one? Theoretically that could happen, although it wasn't likely. Could I admit that I didn't have one, explain my reasons, and count on her understanding and compassion?

Back up against the wall and not trusting my persuasiveness, I said, "It's a Garcia." I do own a Garcia — I just didn't bring it with me.

A few minutes later I walked out of the Wilderness Center, permit in hand. It felt great to have the last hurdle jumped, but oddly discomfiting as well because it wasn't a permit that allowed me to stick to my game plan. Even if my brain hadn't yet accepted it, my heart knew that I was going to leave tomorrow morning and blow right past Little Yosemite Valley, regardless of what was written on the paper I clutched. I had also just lied to the ranger about having a bear can, and I wasn't proud of that fact. These regulations are in place for a reason, and I have respect for those reasons and for the people who walk the thin green line and enforce them. Heck, I have an undergraduate degree in environmental studies! They may seem insignificant in the grand scheme of things, but I will always be slightly ashamed and embarrassed by these indiscretions.

Despite this incongruence, I charged forward, reminding myself that:

1) I had talked to a famous adventurer and fast packer that told me none of the "Big Guns" use bear canisters.
2) I strongly believe that people who are willing to occasionally color outside the lines pave the road to success.
3) I wasn't hurting anyone, I would tread lightly, and there was no way a bear would get my food.

Years ago I had used rationalization to talk myself off the trail, and here I was using it for "good". Perhaps slightly misguided, but that was progress. When it came down to it, my determination to succeed in this moment was like a locomotive with no brakes, and I simply wasn't willing to be derailed.

By now it was early afternoon, and I made my way to the Yosemite Backpacker's Camp. Tucked away behind the horse stables, this small campsite is first-come, first-served and designed for backpackers who are either just starting or just finishing their treks. I have met some fantastically eccentric and interesting people over the years at camps like this, including two wandering spirits who basically live in the wilderness. That night our camp was full, but I stayed to myself, choosing to conserve my energy for what was to come. I set up camp, made dinner, and then just waited. I felt a strange mixture of calm giddiness, almost like a leaf twirling in the undercurrents beneath the surface, still and serene.

"I wonder if he's using the same wind we are using..."

I think there is much to be said about the simple power of
perseverance and determination. The willingness to be in action
and do whatever it takes to get where you want to go can make
up for almost any shortcoming. I know many ultra successful
people who aren't particularly intelligent, charming, or outwardly
unique. You'd meet them and think, "This guy is a millionaire?"
But what they have that most people don't is an unrelenting will to
keep pushing forward, despite obstacles and skeptics. The world
if full of "sayers" — these people are doers. I try to remember this
principle when I feel inadequate or afraid — if I just keep moving, I
will get somewhere.

I had my cell phone (and there is coverage in Yosemite Valley. I
appreciated it at the time but don't think I'll ever be fully on board
with technology intruding into all aspects of our lives) but was
trying to conserve the battery, so I waited as long as I could to call
Jen for the last time. I finally wandered off into the darkness and
dialed her number. No answer. I tried again a few minutes later,
and she answered but couldn't really hear me or communicate
because she was at a concert with a friend. Oh well. I was out
there on my own, and it was time to lock it down emotionally and
put my game face on.

Just as I started drifting off to sleep, a barking laugh jolted me
awake. Then there was another jarring laugh that sounded
inappropriately close to me. I rolled over and discovered that a
group of hikers had stumbled in after dark, set up camp 10 feet
from me, and decided that a bonfire and beer was the perfect way
to end their day, despite the slumbering backpackers surrounding
them. In hindsight I could have approached them, explained my

plight, and asked them to quiet down. I could have thrown sadness, anger, desperation, or logic at them. I could have done many things. But what I decided to do was just "be". To trust that no matter how much sleep I managed to get, tomorrow would be perfect; to not let a drunk group of idiots cloud my thoughts or my mood just when I needed them to be on point more than ever.

Blocking out their intrusion actually proved to be a blessing in disguise. It forced me to actively think about why I was there and to take a mental step back to appreciate the long road that had led to that moment. I let the images and feelings accumulated from hours of training wash over me — and then at some point I eventually found sleep.

Chapter 4
Launch

(Day 1 - Happy Isles to Lyell Headwaters, 35 miles)

"To find your limits you must be willing to test them."
— Jen Mathe

From faraway I heard a muffled beeping, and for a second I had no idea where I was. Then my senses awoke, and I smiled as I turned off my watch alarm. I quickly pulled on clothes and then had something to eat. I often have trouble forcing myself to eat before big events because the butterflies in my stomach are too numerous and kinetic, but on this morning they were still. Anxious to get started I shoveled down breakfast without tasting it, but then slowed down to savor one last coconut water that I'd saved for that moment. Still in the dark, I broke down and packed my sleeping gear by touch, having already memorized the shapes and textures. I could hear the soft murmurs and scrapes of the other backpackers as they engaged in their own morning rituals. In a way we were all connected in a dance of sorts, lost in our own hopes and fears, but moving to the same music.

I cinched my pack tightly (since I was planning to move with speed and agility, I wanted my gear to be an extension of my body), set it on my shoulders, and strode out of camp. I distinctly remember looking back once with a half-smile and nod, a brief acknowledgement that the next time I set foot in this place I would be changed.

As I passed the stables I broke into a jog. A couple of the horses looked up and nickered at me, their breath pluming in the pre-dawn air. I found myself wondering if the beasts were wishing me luck or warning me, and even as I thought this I laughed silently at myself for my need to make meaning from the meaningless. No matter. Luck was something invented by the ill-prepared. I was ready. Not only was I ready, I was so excited to pit myself against all the challenges I would face over the next week and to see what I was made of.

I stopped to take a picture of the trail sign that read "Mount Whitney via John Muir Trail, 211 miles," recorded a short video journal, and then looked down at the trail and scuffed it with my feet. I actually recited Lao Tsu's famous words to myself: "A journey of a thousand miles must begin with a single step." I only had to go 211. Bonus. Looking around slowly, I savored the keen expectation that only belongs to beginnings and took my first step onto the JMT. (The sign read 211 miles because there are varying accounts of the exact length of the John Muir Trail – I've seen it listed as low as 210 and as high as 215. But who's counting right?)

The trail would immediately lead some 5,000 feet straight up out of the valley and over Cathedral Pass, so it seemed prudent to begin with a brisk hike instead of a run. As I started moving, I took a few deep breaths, absorbing the moment and feeling alive. It was cold, which falls right in my wheelhouse. All endurance athletes have their bag of tricks — certain conditions or skills that give them an edge (or make them feel as if they have an edge which is equally as important). Some people like hills, others prefer heat or wind. I excel as the temperature drops. Not that it's comfortable necessarily, but I have such a brightly burning internal furnace that frigid conditions keep my core temperature down and allow me to work harder without overheating.

Pacing is always challenging and is actually one of the harde
most important components of the maturation process of a
You don't want to start too hard and fizzle out before the end. Nor
do you want to go too easy and leave your best on the table. Jen
and I often discuss the misadventures of our less-experienced
athletes with amusement and understanding as we remember
our own pacing mishaps. For this trip, I didn't really know what to
expect in this arena, but I had been training for ultra running, and I
planned to run as much of this trail as I could. I was thinking I'd run
till lunchtime, take a siesta in the shade during the mid-day heat,
and then continue running till just before dark.

After I got warmed up I tried running a couple times and immediately
realized that my initial plan would have to be adjusted — at least
until I was better acclimated. The combination of the weight on my
back and the altitude caused my heart rate to rev too high whenever
I would attempt to run, and I knew I wouldn't be able to sustain that
all day, every day for a week. So for now, it would have to be a fast
hike. That's okay. As Dori from *Finding Nemo* so wisely said, "Just
keep swimming." (Nerdy perhaps, but I actually use this mantra
quite a bit during tough endurance efforts.)

Legs and lungs feeling strong, I ascended quickly. A group of
CrossFit athletes on a day hike to Half Dome had begun just in front
of me, and I took quiet pride in dropping them almost instantly. They
could probably take me back to their gym and Olympic lift me till
I cried uncle, but the John Muir Trail was my domain. I passed a
couple other groups of day hikers and was encouraged. Even if I
wasn't running, my pace seemed to be getting the job done.

Before I knew it I was in Little Yosemite Valley. Having made my
decision the night before, I didn't even slow down as I passed the
campsites and ranger station. The trail had recently leveled out, and

I'd been enjoying the brief respite, but just as quickly I was climbing steep switchbacks once more. As the turnoff to Half Dome neared, I passed a growing number of people who were poorly prepared for this endeavor. Half Dome is one of the few real wonders of the world, and people come from every corner of the Earth to attempt to reach the top and drink in Yosemite Valley from above. But reading about Half Dome in a guidebook doesn't mean it's a good idea to pit oneself against it — a reality many people learn the hard way (even occasionally with their lives).

As I turned a blind corner, my Spidey senses tingled. I thought, "I wonder if a ranger is on the trail and if my permit will be checked?" Sure enough, standing less than a pitch to home plate away was a tall ranger blocking the trail. She had an iPad (insert indignant head shake here) and was checking permits. Gulp. I technically wasn't supposed to be this far on the trail until tomorrow.

"Good morning. Do you have a permit?" she asked with an easy smile. Most rangers I've met are humble and friendly, as if they know how awesome their jobs are and don't want to rub it in.

"Yep. Here you go," I said, handing her my permit. "This should be interesting," I thought to myself.

She swiped her finger down the iPad a few times, brow furrowing. "I don't see you on here. You're hiking Half Dome right?"

"Oh! No, I'm hiking straight through to Whitney. Been to Half Dome and don't want to take the time and effort today!" I exclaimed, perhaps a bit too exuberantly, as I realized she was just enforcing the new permitting regulations for Half Dome and was about to let me continue on my way.

"Well okay then. Have fun!" she said, refolding my permit and giving it back to me. Then she stepped aside and opened her left palm toward the trail as if she were the doorman welcoming me to the Emerald City.

"I guess this whole trip is kind of an existential Wizard of Oz after all," I thought. "Hopefully no flying monkeys. Although I might pray for ruby slippers before this is all over."

Odd musings like these were not uncommon as my brain adapted to being alone, and while they were alarming at first, I grew to enjoy the process and often amused myself to the point of laughter.

The trail soon became even steeper, and all of a sudden reality washed over me; a wave that will always come but the where and when is a mystery. My thoughts went like this: This part was hard. I wasn't Superman. And I would be doing this for a really, really long time. Then I listened for the answering cascade of negative voices, but there was only sweet silence. These realities were true, however it was also true that I was enjoying the oneness and effort and still looking forward to the looming unknown.

Eventually I lost myself for a while in the flow of movement and breath. (This is a natural process that happens to most long-distance runners during some or all of their runs, and I would spend countless hours over the next week immersed in this moving meditation of extreme calm and focus). After the left turn to Half Dome the trail emptied, and for the first time I was able to truly revel in the vastness surrounding me and the strange euphoria stimulated by feeling completely dwarfed by but connected to everything.

Eyes turned inward, I was surprised to find a figure just ahead, moving quickly in a small dust cloud of his own.

"Morning!" I offered as I scooted past him on the narrow path.

He smiled wearily and gave me a barely perceptible nod. Then he stopped hiking and shifted his pack to a more comfortable position.

In the unwritten annals of trail etiquette, it is considered good form to stop and chat briefly with other backpackers you meet along the trail (which also happens to offer a fantastic excuse for taking a break, so almost everyone does it).

"You doing the whole JMT?" I asked, taking in his gargantuan pack and the determined look in his eyes.

"That's the plan," he replied, nodding. "Hoping to do it in seven days, but this pack is already feeling heavy. You're pack is tiny. You're not doing the whole thing are you?"

"Actually I am. I'm going as light and fast as I can."

We talked for a few more minutes and then I kept moving. This interaction was the first of many that were nearly identical. Appreciation for the rest, and for the harmony of two voices breaking the silence; slight awe and incredulousness at the size of my pack and speed with which I was moving; and the warmth of human contact. I came to look forward to these brief connections, particularly as I thought about how unique they were in the grand scheme of things. Two people coming together for a fleeting instant, sharing the intimacy of common purpose, and then turning back to the jagged rock, alone.

Eventually I made my way over Cathedral Pass and was rewarded by my first real downhill of the day. Looking at the map I knew the hard part was over and I was feeling confident, so I broke into a trot. The combination of weight on my back, steep terrain, and gravity took some getting used to, but within minutes I was careening downhill with a grin plastered to my face. There is something immensely satisfying about running point-to-point (versus out and back) and covering ground you will never have to see again — particularly when you're doing it with reckless abandon.

Downhill running isn't nearly as challenging to your cardiovascular system, but it is by no means easy. I was extremely thankful for my training and found myself acutely aware on many occasions of the broken ankles or dangerous falls I would have had without the proprioception and strength I had built. Also, the repeated, jolting impact and need to constantly decelerate takes a toll on the joints and muscles. It was with all this in mind that I finally skidded to a stop and decided to have lunch.

I had grown accustomed to the sound of the wind whistling in my ears and the slap of my shoes on the dirt, and when I stopped the silence was almost overwhelming. I un-slung my pack and ran some internal diagnostics. I realized I was tired, nauseous, and had the beginnings of a fairly substantial headache. My mental training was proving itself. As I ate I thought about how years before any of these factors could easily have dampened my spirits and begun the negative siren song. But now I was showing grit and resiliency and doing so with a practiced hand. Pain, fatigue, and discomfort — these feelings were there, but I was able to casually swat them away as if they were mosquitoes looking for a nice place to touch down on my skin. I simply didn't let them land, and instead focused on the exhilaration of living my passion and (literally) running toward my goals.

After 30 minutes (my detail-oriented coach/wife will be pleased to know I actually set an alarm) of food and rest, I felt much more human. As a nutritionist I was virtually certain that my physical symptoms were largely due to malnourishment, however knowing and doing are markedly different things. This would be an issue for me during the entire trip, and I struggled for a few reasons:

- I was in the "Zone" and didn't want to take myself out of it to eat.
- I wasn't feeling particularly hungry or thirsty.
- I didn't want to take the time to eat.

(I quickly decided to put small snacks in the accessible front pouches of my pack so I could eat while moving, and this helped quite a bit.)

Back on the move, I continued making steady progress as the trail gently rolled. I found a rhythm of fast hiking the uphill sections, running the downhill areas, and alternating between walking and jogging on the flats. Presently, I was passing Tuolumne Meadows, and I gave silent thanks to my ghost from years ago. I believe it is our darkest times that allow us perspective, and that without them we would not be able to fully appreciate the bright spots. It is for this reason that I am deeply grateful for and humbled by all the younger, sillier versions of me.

Barley is nothing without the hops

I could be overly sensitive, or maybe it's merely part of the human condition, but the painful times in my life have always affected me deeply. Over time I subconsciously developed rules, strategies, and complex defense mechanisms to avoid the darkness at all costs — and of course I have still taken some monumental stumbles that have cracked my armor and left me bloody and broken. These falls were terrible, and I won't pretend otherwise, but after dusting myself off and looking back I have to admit it is these times more than any others that have propelled me toward growth and happiness. The protective walls still stand, but acknowledging and appreciating the entire spectrum of life experience is an important step. My castle now has a drawbridge and front gate ... and one of these days I'll knock the walls down completely.

As the shadows grew long my energy began slowly dropping like the sun in the sky. I was nearing the 30-mile mark for the day and had been moving almost continuously for 10 hours. I had made it to the heart of Lyell Canyon, and I was surrounded by the picturesque beauty often associated with the high sierras — lush meadows, split by a sparkling river, framed against massive, toothed peaks. It was enough that on more than one occasion I slowed to shake my head in wonder and appreciation. The terrain was also consistently flat for once, however I wasn't able to summon the reserves necessary to run. I acknowledged some slight frustration at this reality, however I chose to avoid the rabbit hole and instead focus on the fact that I had only five miles left to travel. I would just move as fast as I could manage and that would be enough.

It was during this mental gyration that I suddenly found myself trotting behind someone. Even from behind I could tell he was different than anyone else I had seen thus far. He was compact and slender and sported trail-running shoes instead of the clunky boots favored by most backpackers. His pack was bigger than mine, but he moved with speed and grace. Finally as I got closer I noticed his Boston Marathon shirt, and my assumptions were confirmed. I had found another runner. This may seem insignificant, but at the time it was like touching a piece of home.

"Hey! I haven't seen anybody else crazy enough to wear shoes like that!" I said enthusiastically.

He turned, smiled wryly, and said, "Yeah, I'm carrying enough weight, and I didn't want to carry any more on my feet."

We hiked and talked. His name was Demian, a lawyer from LA, out here attempting the whole JMT on his own after a buddy bailed at the last minute. Even though he'd never really done any backpacking before, he decided to come anyway and see what he was made of. We chatted about running, women, and life, and before I knew it we had covered three or four miles.

The company and slightly slower pace had given me a second wind, and my stomach began grumbling. We decided to stop for dinner, and when he offered to share his meal I nodded with enthusiastic thanks. I had learned long ago to graciously accept any and all food offered in the backcountry. Why? Gifted food represents precious calories that I don't have to purchase or carry, and allows me to keep the food I already have as a reserve against the unknown. We used a flat rock as a cutting board and carved heaping chunks of Parmesan cheese and salami that we wrapped into large flour tortillas. It was an odd pairing for sure, but I've never had a better burrito. The whole episode filled me with amused contentment as well because Demian had fastidiously researched the best weight-to-calorie ratios and decided that this threesome was the ideal dinner combination. It reminded me of something Jen or my friend John would do, and it was the emotional equivalent of coming inside from a blizzard to find a warm fire crackling in the hearth. Once again I was reminded that it was good to be alone and to be exploring the wild both outside and within me — but only in contrast to simple human connection and the wonderfully mundane bric-a-brac that decorates my life.

Over dinner we discussed our plans moving forward. He was carrying considerably more weight than I was, and aimed to complete the trail in two to three weeks. We agreed to continue hiking until dusk, make camp, and then begin tomorrow's adventure together. I would quickly outpace him at that point, but we both liked the idea of warding off the loneliness as long as we could. Even on day one (day two for Demian) we had already developed an almost reverent respect for the power of loneliness.

It was always there, like a waterfall cascading to the depths below. We could hear the thundering crashes if we stopped to listen, but mostly it was just there on the fuzzy edges of perception, dangerous and beautiful.

I couldn't tell exactly where we were on my map when we finally decided to stop, but we were close enough to Lyell Headwaters and my 35-mile goal to call it a day. We crossed a slick log and found ourselves on a small meadow island. I treasure the simplicity of backcountry life, and as I began the familiar routine of setting up camp, I released some tension that I hadn't been aware of till that moment. This had been an exceptional day. Already my physical and mental preparation had been tested and emerged with high marks. I had also managed to hit my target distance for the day, despite not being able to run as much as I had anticipated. Lastly, I'd met a kindred spirit who added an unexpected richness to the experience. Yes, this was an entirely different trip, and so far it had been everything I was hoping for and then some.

Chapter 5
The Bear

"Life inevitably throws us curve balls, unexpected circumstances that remind us to expect the unexpected. I've come to understand these curve balls are the beautiful unfolding of both karma and current."
— Carre Otis

I was jolted awake by angry shouting in the dark. As I came fully alert I realized there was only one plausible explanation. A bear must have wandered into a nearby campsite looking for food. I mouthed a silent curse. Yosemite bears are notoriously crafty and tenacious, and I was really hoping to pass through unnoticed. I was confident that my food was safe as I had stuffed it in a nylon sack and hung it from a branch 15 feet above ground, however I had no desire to tempt fate; although, given the circumstances that had led me here it somehow seemed karmically perfect that a bear had suddenly entered the equation.

"Josh, did you hear that?" Demian's voice asked in the dark.

"Yep. There's probably a bear in that campsite we passed before crossing the river. Hopefully he just stays over there," I replied, trying to keep the anxiety out of my voice.

Demian had his food in a bear canister sitting in the middle of the field next to us, so ostensibly his food would be safe no matter how curious this bear was. However, we had both been warned that Yosemite bears had been known to break into bear canisters if given enough time, so Demian decided to pull on some clothes and stand watch. He stood huddled next to the perceived safety of his tent, headlight slowly rotating and piercing the blackness like a sentinel lighthouse. After a few minutes of complete silence, he retreated to the warmth of his sleeping bag once more. We decided the bear was probably using the trail as the easiest passage down the valley and that he'd either found food or kept moving.

As I lay there trying to find sleep once more, it occurred to me how difficult it must be for a soldier to drop his guard enough to sleep restfully. Despite my best efforts to relax, my body was tingling and my ears were straining to catch the slightest crack of a twig or rustle of underbrush. And like a soldier, my shelter only gave the illusion of protection. I have always harbored a strong respect for bears in the wild because they can run, climb, and swim faster than I can. They are stronger, hungrier, and can smell a body from miles away. When you're out there in the dark you tell yourself that California brown bears are basically just big raccoons that don't generally hurt humans, but that doesn't fully quiet the primal voice that simply doesn't want to be eaten alive. It is a deep, elemental feeling, and it's sobering to think about the lives our ancestors lived and how this voice was born.

At this point sleep seemed as far away as the dawn, and I couldn't help but think back on my past bear encounters. Brief flashes of brown in my peripheral vision. Being flanked for a couple miles in the Trinity Alps. An unfortunate episode in Kings Canyon where I was taking care of "business" and a small bear walked right in front of me, startling me so much that I jumped backward into said "business". I smiled as these innocuous memories trickled through my mind. But then my brain found what it was looking for, and I was instantly transported to that night 15 years ago and roughly 30 miles from this very spot.

I was on a backpacking trip with my dad, sister, and girlfriend. It was a long hike in, and by the time we arrived at our destination none of us had the energy to engage in the manual labor of making camp. We pitched tents, shared a couple of freeze-dried meals, half-heartedly hung our food, and crashed. In the morning we found our food spread all over camp. While some of it was gone or destroyed, much of it was still edible. Apparently a bear had easily plucked it out of the tree (it was only six feet off the ground — we may as well have put it on a platter), selected the choicest morsels, and moved on. A little wake-up call, embarrassing, but not the end of the world. We decided to move a few miles up the canyon and simply survive on a little less food.

The next night my Dad and I vowed to outsmart the bear, and we managed to snag our food on an arching branch at least 30-feet high. We used an enormous stick to carefully place it so there wasn't even a rope for the bear to slice or pull on. Confident in our wiliness, we went to bed.

The night was freezing and silent; but then just as I was drifting off to sleep I heard what could only be our food bag falling to the ground. A bear (probably the same one) must have shaken the tree hard enough to dislodge the bag from the branch. "Unbelievable," I thought to myself. I should have forced myself to confront the bear; to face my fears and go forth despite them. Or at the very least call out to my dad. But instead I lay there, constrained by chains of terror and shame, and listened to the bear eat all of our food. We hiked out the next morning, hungry but no worse for wear. None of my trip mates seemed to have an issue with my inaction, but I judged myself. I was appalled by what this moment said about me, and I vowed to react differently if ever given a similar opportunity.

Now, so many years and experiences later, I found myself praying for the bear to move on ... and yet also desperately hoping he would enter my arena and battle. I chased these conflicting thoughts and emotions till I was finally far enough away to find sleep.

"Zzzzzp."

My eyes were open in a flash. I looked down at my watch and pressed the button to illuminate it: 12:52 a.m. A little less than an hour since Demian had abandoned watch. I tried to mentally recreate the sound that had just awoken me. It sounded like a synthetic material being ripped or sliding quickly along wood. Either way, it most likely meant my food was in jeopardy and that whether I was ready or not the chance to rewrite history was upon me. For an infinitesimal second I considered pulling the quilt over my head, closing my eyes tight, and rocking back and forth like *Rainman* until I was magically teleported home to warmth and safety. But then I took a long, deep breath and steeled myself. It was time to take action.

"Demian. You awake?" I shouted, both to wake up Demian and let the bear know it wasn't alone.

"Yeah Josh. I heard it too. What do you want to do?" he replied.

"It sounded like the bear has my food or will have it soon, so I'm getting up to stop him. You in?"

Stating my intentions infused me with purpose, and while by no means comforting it was empowering to be proactive.

"Sure man, let's do this," Demian sounded about as excited as I felt.

He was grateful we had run into each other on the trail, and he had admitted that as an inexperienced backpacker nighttime in the Sierras spooked him a bit. But to his credit he crawled out of his tent and stood beside me to brave the unknown.

We stumbled through a dry-creek bed and shined our twin headlamps in the direction of the tree that was harboring my food. Twenty feet away two shining eyes glared back at us. It was a bear, a big one, and it was standing directly under the spot I'd hung my food. I shifted my gaze higher so that the light illuminated the tree, and a wave of relief swept over me as I saw my food bag hanging right where I'd left it. The noise that had jerked me from sleep must have been the rope shifting. My food was still there, and if I could simply drive the beast away all would be well.

We began yelling nonsensical obscenities and waving our arms. This is usually enough to get a bear to clear out, either out of fear or more likely confusion at the stupidity of humans. But this bear simply stood there, staring at us, daring us to come closer. We looked at each other, and then as one reached down to grab handfuls of rocks to lob at the enormous carnivore.

"Is this a good idea?" Demian asked.

I was thinking the same thing. Pissing off a 700-pound mass of teeth and claws that could cover the distance between us in seconds might not be the smartest course of action.

But what I said was, "Totally. He's more afraid of us than we are of him." I hoped I was right.

You've probably heard the saying: You don't have to outrun the bear — you just have to outrun the person next to you. Usually I would be morbidly emboldened by this wisdom, however I already knew Demian was a Boston-qualifying marathon runner so this gave me no solace.

Suddenly Demian scored a direct hit and the bear bolted into the darkness.

"Nice shot, brother!" I whooped.

We took a few steps toward my food, scanned the area with our lights, and then headed back to our tents when we saw nothing further amiss.

This time, sleep came even slower. Every fiber of my being was alight with hyper awareness. In looking back I realize I was in the same "Zone" commonly associated with sports or sex. When the world narrows and all purpose and passion is pointed at what is directly in front of you. It was partially for instances like these that I was drawn to this trail, so the Universe was giving me what I'd asked for — albeit with a different twist than I was expecting.

Morning came without further incident. It was unseasonably frigid, and the twilight just before dawn is always coldest; so though awake, I remained huddled in my quilt with only my beanie-capped head protruding as the sky slowly lightened. Living without real shelter for days on end offers a unique perspective and connection to the natural world. Temperature and light become tangible forces that shape decisions, influence mood, and provide succor or suffering. Eventually I unzipped my tent and stepped into the freshness of the new day. I rolled my shoulders and turned my head from side-to-side to work out the kinks that always come from a night spent on the ground. Then I strolled to a nearby tree to relieve myself and marveled at the billowing steam I was creating. Why is it that certain things never cease to capture our wonder and imagination? I have to admit I find pee-steam fascinating, just as I will stare awestruck at down-pouring rain. I laughed at myself. Free from the constraints of society my brain was unleashed to solve any of the great mysteries of life, and here I was admiring the magic of my urine.

As I made my way over to my food bag, I instantly noticed that something didn't feel right. The bag was still hanging in the tree, but in the morning light it looked lifeless and vacant. My heart squeezed hard and my scalp tingled as stress endorphins shot through me. Walking closer, it became obvious that we had tragically misinterpreted the situation the night before. My food bag was swaying listlessly in the soft wind, empty, a clean cut right across the bottom. The ground below was littered with the ravaged remains of my food. The carnage cut an impressive swath, and the bear had been hungry and thorough. Nothing remained. In fact many non-edible items were missing, swallowed or stolen by the brute. I stood there for a full minute, frozen in disbelief and slowly creeping dismay. I was so laser-focused on completing this trip that my brain didn't know what to do with this new information. For those first few moments I was quite literally incapable of accepting this new reality in which I may not be able to keep moving forward.

I stumbled back to camp in a fog, directionless, and without answers. Demian was hunched over his stove and looked up at me, eyes widening as he saw my face.

"Bear got my food after all. He must have climbed the tree, stuck a claw out, cut the bottom of the bag, and then feasted all night while we slept. We had such a hard time driving him away because he was guarding my food — his food. We just didn't get close enough to see the food on the ground," I said numbly.

"Josh, that's sucks. I'm so sorry, man. What are you going to do?"

"I don't know, Demian," I replied, reality just beginning to peek through the static in my head.

"There's really no way you can keep going is there?" he asked, ever the pragmatic lawyer.

There it was: It was as if the words hung in the air, suspended until I dared look at them. And when I looked, life came rushing back like a massive "play" button had just been pushed.

"No, there really isn't. That was all my food until my resupply, two full days and 80 miles from here. I told my wife and Mom I wouldn't do anything stupid out here and trying to make that resupply would definitely be stupid," I said.

Part of me wanted to test myself against those odds and to refuse to accept the changed circumstances, but a larger part of me knew what I had just said was pure truth. Jen and I have talked on more than one occasion about the nuance between being tenacious and being stubborn. There is a small but important difference, and it's one that plays a key role in endurance sport.

Tenacious: tending to keep a firm hold of something; clinging or adhering closely.

Stubborn: having or showing dogged determination not to change one's attitude or position on something, in spite of good arguments or reasons to do so.

Both states of being fan the fire that pushes you toward your goals, but only tenacity allows for adaptability. It is a key step in the maturation process of an athlete to accept that there are times when changing course is the best option. This was absolutely one of those times.

"I think my best move is to hike back the 10 miles to Tuolumne Meadows where I can get some food and catch a bus back to my car in Yosemite Valley," I said with more confidence than I'd had all morning.

This was the right move — it was the only move, and I was exceedingly lucky it was even a possibility. If this had happened virtually anywhere else on the trail I would be stuck without food or transportation for many hours or even days.

"Good call. That's what I would do too. I could give you a little food but not enough to make a difference," Demian said. "I would be happy to give you some oatmeal and coffee though."

I accepted Demian's generous offer with a twinge of guilt, but quickly reciprocated by giving him my beanie and gloves. He would be out here for another two weeks and the clothing he had was barely enough to keep him safe in temperatures like this.

While I was deeply frustrated by the new development, having a plan gave me energy for action. I shot a video journal at the site of the "incident" (which you can watch on YouTube. It looks like I'm crying but I swear I was just cold), packed up my gear, and sent Demian on his way after exchanging contact information.

Just as I had the previous morning, I slowly looked back as I walked out of camp. This time I vowed to return, and I nodded with the conviction of this promise.

There is almost no fuel that burns as hot and efficient as anger, and I used mine to reach Tuolumne Meadows in record time (after a slip and full body river submersion just as I was leaving camp. Cold would be the understatement of the century). At Tuolumne I bought snacks and read book pages (I didn't bring a full book because of the weight) in the sun as I waited for the bus that would return me to my car in Yosemite Valley two hours away. My brain proved too active for reading, and I let it wander. I thought about how cool it was that it would take a bus two hours to drive me the distance I had covered on foot in just a day; about how much I had already proven and how proud I should be; about how I would get back and finish what I started.

I tried to work through the logistics of obtaining a bear canister, a bigger pack, and replacement food, while still returning to the trail with enough time to finish and make it back for our Whistler trip. The puzzle pieces just didn't fit. In order to continue my journey I would have to head home and return another time. That stung, but I used the pain to further harden my resolve. Back against cold granite, eyes to the sky, a Yosemite breeze tickling my skin, I reiterated my promise. I didn't know the when or the how, but I would return to this spot; I would set my feet due south; and absolutely nothing would stop me from standing on Whitney in triumph.

Find your sparkplugs and use them

We all have different things that serve as our motivational kindling, and I can tell you that 100 percent of the time my clients who reach their goals are the ones who get extremely honest and specific about what drives them. In this case I was ignited by anger, but that is just one of countless things that may spark you. Know your reasons, define your goals, put them in a place you can see and touch them every day (emotionally and physically), and get excited about seeing them blossom. Don't worry about being perfect — just keep your eye on the prize and commit to moving toward your goals more often than you move away from them.

Chapter 6
Getting Back

"You may encounter many defeats, but you must not be defeated. In fact, it may be necessary to encounter the defeats, so you can know who you are, what you can rise from, how you can still come out of it."
— Maya Angelou

As I drove home from Yosemite I continued to mentally wrestle with my situation. Returning to the JMT this year seemed like a logistical long shot, but the idea of putting it off was repellent. I had trained my body and mind to peak at this moment in time, and I had rearranged my entire world to make this trip happen. I had little desire to depressurize the mechanism and then have to prime the pump all over again. I also burned to finish what I started. My need to conquer and complete the trail was so strong that it was almost a living thing inside me, and I questioned my ability to contain its growth. I imagined this need taking shape and ripping me open in gruesome fashion (yes, I like the movie *Alien*). While I knew this was fantastical, I truly questioned my facility to remain balanced and productive while mired in this uncomfortable purgatory.

After returning home I decided to give myself a couple days "off" and deliberately focused on other areas of my life that fed my purpose and passion.

Take one step back and then two steps forward

I find this is often the best way to solve a problem; kick around ideas for a while and then step back and invest energy elsewhere. Do something fun and completely different. If you enjoy creating things, dive into that for a few days. This offers fresh perspective and motivation when ready to return to the issue, and it allows your subconscious mind to work in the background like a passive problem-solving program. Have you ever tangled with a problem during the day, moved on, and then woken up the next morning with a solution? That's your subconscious mind doing its job well, and sometimes the best way to harness this power is to simply step out of the way.

A little distance from my dilemma proved to be just what I needed, and when I sat down to hatch a plan it came easily and naturally. Like I had done previously when first planning the trip, I made a list of everything I would need to figure out in order to return to the trail and finish it successfully:

- Bear-proofing
- Timing and permit
- Physical and mental preparation
- Client coverage
- Changed weather conditions

BEAR-PROOFING

This was at the top of my list for obvious reasons. If I couldn't figure out how to keep my food away from bears, I might as well stay home. The good news is that I knew what I had to do. The John Muir Trail winds through multiple wilderness areas and jurisdictions, and all of them either require or strongly suggest a bear canister. I had consciously chosen not to bring a bear can the first time because I didn't want to carry the extra weight or a pack big enough to hold one. In researching for this second attempt I realized my bias was mostly overblown, and that I could solve the problem with a very small addition of weight and bulk. I purchased the smallest, lightest bear canister on the market (Lil Sami by Lighter 1, 1 lb 12 oz). I was also able to find the exact same pack I already had, but with 7 L more volume (OMM Classic Marathon 32L, 1 lb 4 oz — only 4 oz heavier than the smaller one). I bought food for the trip, and stuffed it into the bear canister to make sure there would be enough room (keeping in mind that when I picked up my resupply the can would have to fit three days of food). It would be tight, but if I channeled my inner Tetris-master it worked. Bear problem solved.

TIMING AND PERMIT

Due to our previous travel commitments and a 40th anniversary party for my parents the soonest I would be able to restart my trip was the middle of September (a little over a month). While this frustrated me, the reality was that I would probably need that time to find an open permit window, and it would give me an opportunity to reconnect with my clients. When I checked with the Tuolumne Wilderness Center my suspicions were confirmed — the first day that had any permits available was Monday, September 16. I was hoping to begin on a weekend to minimize work time off, but I was not about to look a gift horse in the mouth and was acutely aware of my luck to find any permits available at all! I happily reserved a permit to be picked up in person on Sunday afternoon, September 15.

PHYSICAL AND MENTAL PREPARATION

This may seem like a no-brainer since I was already prepared and would now have another month to train. However my bones, joints, muscles, and cardiovascular system had endured hundreds of punishing miles over the course of the year and were perfectly tuned to optimally synergize for my first attempt. Now I would have to walk a fine line of staying conditioned without overtraining that would lead to debilitating fatigue or injury.

After consulting with Jen I decided to take the remainder of that first week off from running and fully recharge my body and spirit. Then I would run often but keep my mileage fairly low for a couple weeks, and finish with more volume and intensity to ramp back up for another peak (if possible) mid-September. In terms of brain training, I would continue my daily practices (visualizing hope, belief, and a successful second attempt) while still living in the moment. I didn't want to go through the motions for a month and miss the rest of my life simply because I was caught in a self-imposed holding pattern.

The road trip to Whistler proved to be a blessing in disguise and helped solidify my core belief that circumstances unfold the way they do for a reason and that there are opportunities for growth and joy in all things. Unlike the usual mad dash to a race, we decided to take three days to drive to Whistler, enjoying each other and friends along the way. It was connecting and fun, and greatly rejuvenated me on many levels.

I am eternally grateful that I get to spend all day helping people become happier and healthier. What I do on a fundamental level is facilitate people finding and embracing the strongest, truest versions of who they are. I love it, and it nourishes my soul in a way I can't fully describe. I know Jen feels similarly. The darker, less visible side of this is that we both spend vast amounts of time and energy on our business. We work for ourselves and can set our own schedules, but this often means we are working until the wee hours every night of the week. It also means that unless we catch ourselves and actively choose not to, most of our interaction and communication is about our business. This Whistler trip was a

You are here

It's insidiously easy to become so focused on where you want
to go that you forget to look at where you are, isn't it? We
think we'll be happy or fulfilled when ... the book is finished,
the mountain is climbed, the degree is completed, the ring
is offered. But of course that's ridiculous and completely
discounts all the moments leading up to those things. Striving
is an integral part of the human experience, but so is being.
When I can (which is not all the time) I try to remember to take
my eyes off the horizon and look at the ground I'm standing on,
as well as the ground I've already covered. Otherwise I'll be
waiting to "arrive" forever ...

welcome opportunity to simply relish being together, and it anchored
me at a time I could easily have become adrift.

I soon discovered that Whistler also happens to be a trail running
Mecca! Between the hiking trails, mountain biking trails, and
cross-country skiing trails (that were designed for the 2010 Winter
Olympics) there are hundreds of miles of single-track nirvana
weaving through the picturesque mountain landscape. My last few
weeks of training for the JMT had worn on me almost like a job,
and the bear had robbed my trip of some enchantment, but flying
through the Whistler wilderness reminded me how much I love to
run. There were crazy, rolling footbridges that looked like they had
been designed by Disney for some Middle Earth adventure, and
every trail had a clever name like "Pinocchio's Staircase" or "Dwarf
Nebula". I ran every day we were there, usually with my shirt off
(even when it rained), and couldn't wait to feel the wind and wet on
my skin. I ran fast, slow, up, down, and got lost in the easy fluidity
of movement. It was like my own amusement park, and I can't

remember ever feeling so alive or having so much fun. In short (or in long — sometimes I get carried away when talking about this stuff), it was exactly what I needed, exactly when I needed it.

Was my body ideally peaked for the return to the JMT? Maybe. Probably not. But it didn't matter. It was close enough, and we did our best with the circumstances presented to us. I knew then what I knew on my first trip — my body would not be the limiting factor. I felt a calm strength in knowing that my brain wouldn't hold me back either as this hiatus had put me in an even better mental and emotional space than before.

CLIENT COVERAGE

This is not an exciting read and I won't spend much time on it, however it was an integral part of my ability to go on either JMT attempt, and I'd like to acknowledge the individuals who stepped in to help, and my clients for championing me with grace and selflessness. My clients put great trust in me, and I wear that responsibility with pride and gravity. I was not comfortable deciding to go back to the mountains to fulfill my own deep need to test myself until I was certain that everyone was on the right track and that no progress would be stunted. Knowing that competent people were tending my garden and that my clients heartily supported my efforts buoyed me and gave me peace. Thank you to all who made this possible.

CHANGED WEATHER CONDITIONS

One of my primary concerns when considering returning to the JMT in 2013 was based on my assumption that I wouldn't be able to avoid snow and the pitfalls associated with it (namely extreme cold and disappearing trails). While California's High Sierras are known for their temperance relative to other mountain ranges, the weather is still wildly unpredictable and can become uncomfortable or dangerous within minutes; and there is a small optimal window between the summer snowmelt and autumn snowfall. However in researching and talking to backpacking aficionados it became clear that September is generally on par with August, except with colder average temperatures. Deep snow is rare, and I would probably avoid snow altogether.

There is almost nothing worse than being cold in the wild. It chases and punishes you with quiet, unrelenting persistence until your bones hurt and you begin to fantasize about saunas and lava fields. Having experienced this torture on more than one occasion, I grudgingly added a few items to my pack list to account for the colder climate:

- Silk sleeping-bag liner — weighs ounces and is supposed to raise sleeping temperature by 5-10 degrees.
- Light, synthetic vest — would serve as a middle layer between my jacket and thermal shirt. I chose synthetic instead of down because it was only an ounce heavier and would still perform when wet with sweat or rain.
- Replacement gloves and beanie (remember, I gave the others to Demian) — both from Mizuno's Breath Thermo line — they generate heat by capturing evaporating sweat. I don't know exactly how this magic happens, but they work.

As September 16th drew near a potential roadblock reared its head: A once-in-a-generation wildfire was sweeping through Yosemite, and all roads to Tuolumne were closed. Containment was days or weeks away and even then highway closures and air quality would be major concerns. If I had to abandon my first attempt because of a hungry bear only to have my second attempt thwarted by a fire it would be frustrating and maddening. I tried not to give any mental energy to this development and instead focus on elements I could control. Since I could do nothing about the fire I chose to trust (the word "chose" is important here) that my path would be clear and the air would be breathable, because letting go and giving myself to belief was the only way I could manage my anxiety.

I called the Tuolumne Wilderness Center two days before I was set to leave and found my faith rewarded. The roads had opened that morning, and the air quality was better than expected as the winds were blowing the smoke north. I smiled and reflected on this news and how I had known it would be so before I even made the call. Did I manifest this reality with my mind, causing winds to change and firefighters to work harder? I doubt it. But there is something miraculous and unexplainable that happens when you can see your destination with stark clarity and know with conviction that you will get there. Belief is powerful medicine.

Sunday arrived, and I quietly gathered my things and loaded the car. The final hours before leaving for my first JMT attempt had been thick with the electricity of the unknown and a lifetime event almost arrived. This time I was all cool determination and business-like efficiency. I knew what to expect, and I would calmly walk the length of the diving board till it was time to jump in with abandon.

Late that afternoon I drove into Tuolumne Meadows under a pristine, smokeless sky. A month ago this area had been alive with summer bustle, but now there were only a few visitors milling around. I quickly obtained my permit without incident, bought some dinner items at the local store (that was closing for the season the next day), and retired to the backpacker's camp for the evening.

Like last time, I had a period of a few hours before bed to fully transition to Josh the ultra-endurance athlete and slowly remove all the other hats I wear. All athletes do this, consciously or subconsciously, and my process has evolved over time. What I did this evening was simply a continuation of the work I'd been doing all year. I took a short jog to stretch out my legs and ended at a river where I sat and appreciated the crash of the water against the rocks. I meditated, sitting comfortably, eyes closed, and thought about how grateful I was to be in this moment, how much I love my wife, and how deeply fulfilling my life is. I saw the trail in my mind, and felt the rush of adrenaline as I crested every pass. Reserved and almost distant all day, the excitement began to bubble to the surface. Even as I write this I feel the same giddy exuberance, and it's all I can do not to run outside and scream a war cry. It was time.

Chapter 7
A Gift in Every Moment

*(Day 2 - Tuolumne Backpackers Camp to
Red Cones, 35 miles)*

*"Always bear in mind that your own resolution to
succeed is more important than any one thing."*
— Abraham Lincoln

Dawn found me on the trail, an hour into an easy jog; body already loose and steaming. I was traveling quickly, but I was oddly disconcerted. Last night had been unusually challenging. A full moon had found its way into my tent through a hole in the tree canopy, and I kept waking up to false sunfall on my closed eyes. A slight melancholy had also begun to take hold in my heart as I thought about being away from Jen and the comforts of home. I am constantly fighting a battle between hard and soft; external and internal. One side of me stands at attention in full battle dress, jaw clenched, fiercely committed to independence; the other side looks up with arms flung wide, caressed by the rays of Jen's light, wanting nothing more than to bury my face in her neck and get lost in her goodness.

Jen is a lightning rod for this turmoil, but it's bigger than her. For most of my life I've fantasized about hiking into some remote backcountry, building a cabin, and living out the rest of my days as a hermit. I used to think the wellspring of this desire was solitude, peace, simplicity, and space to let my mind wander. And while there may be some truth there, I've come to believe the real driving force behind my urge to get lost where I can't be found is safety. If I'm alone, no one can hurt or judge me; I wouldn't have to be perfect, I'd just have to be me. It is encouraging that I no longer feel this way very often, and when I do I generally recognize it as the fleeting, empty promise that it is. The warmer, more open part of me has embraced my very real need for connection. I love to be surrounded by people who see and appreciate me for who I am and to experience the easy camaraderie of shared experience. For some reason I felt this inner struggle keenly the previous night, and it left me with an uneasy hangover.

While contemplating the various forces that drive me was interesting and potentially enlightening, I wanted to fully step into the current experience with a mindset that would maximize success. In an attempt to bring my focus back to the trail I mentally reviewed my updated trip itinerary. Last time I planned to cover the entire 223 miles in six days. This time I started 25 miles into the trail (at Tuolumne, exactly where I had left it), and would be attempting a daunting 198 miles in five days (39.6 miles per day). I was confident my body was capable of such extreme mileage, however I had no idea how long it would actually take me to cover these miles; topographical maps are helpful but only become tangible once you strain to pull every pound of your body and gear up the side of 14,000-foot mountain.

This focusing exercise helped, and I was soon lost in the flow of the trail. Truly a moving meditation, hours would pass in what seemed like minutes. It was noticing this phenomenon years ago that convinced me how powerful my brain could be in determining my performance and enjoyment during endurance sports. While covering the same miles and using the same muscles, my range of perceived experience can vary greatly based on my attitude, expectations, and self-talk. Many triathletes or ultra runners will tell you that it is easier to run for two hours than for 30 minutes. I've experienced this myself. The reason is that we mentally prepare for the longer runs and take the seemingly less significant runs for granted.

Prepare for the short "runs" too

It's not lost on me what an appropriate allegory this is for many things in life, and this awareness has helped make me more effective across the board. To further illustrate the point, here's a typical weekday for me:

5:00 AM — 11:00 AM	Client sessions
11:00 AM — 11:30 PM	Returning emails, phone calls, misc admin
12:00 PM — 1:00 PM	Speaking engagement
1:30 PM — 2:30 PM	Writing
3:00 PM — 4:30 PM	Trail run
4:45 PM — 5:30 PM	Phone consultations
5:30 PM — 6:30 PM	Business meeting
6:30 PM — 7:30 PM	Teaching group class
7:30 PM — 11:00 PM	Relaxing/spending time with Jen, friends, or family

Not all my days are this full and varied, but many of them are. For years I would frantically jump from one activity to the other, carrying all the accumulated daily baggage with me. My energy, focus, and sense of purpose would gradually dwindle until I was ineffective and grumpy. (Notice that my loved ones are at the very end of the day. Not good in this equation!) What I began to see and then hone through endurance sport is that I could employ an easy two-step process to stay energized and engaged all day.

1) Treat each day as an endurance event and mentally prepare for it (as a whole as well as for each activity contained within the event as I would with a triathlon). What activities would require the most energy? What physical preparation would be necessary? Where does it make the most sense to fit that in? (I now try to supercharge this preparation by liberally sprinkling in "energy boosters" like coffee with my cousin or writing with my dad.)

2) When I engage in an activity, I always try to be completely in the moment and give all of myself to it. Leave fears, anger, worries, excitement, etc. about other events until it is appropriate and necessary to look at them.

In short order I reached the back of Lyell Canyon and the fateful spot where my food was devoured by the bear. My eyes narrowed and the wisp of a smile lit my face as a cascade of emotions washed through me — irony, amusement, pride, and determination. I find my goals are often laced with these feelings and almost define my identity. I hold a vast aquifer, filled with both light and dark elements that drive me to prove myself; but separate from that is a more fundamental feeling that I (and maybe everyone) make things much harder than they need to be, and that the fabric that holds us all together is benevolent and has a great sense of humor.

The sun was bright, but the wind was blowing so hard I had to lean against it a few times to avoid being knocked off balance. As a former baseball player I have an ingrained dislike for wind (it just makes everything harder), but on this day it helped keep me cool and gave a shrieking edge to the wild country that added to the immediacy of the experience. I passed two older couples as I really got into the uphill groove, and when I saw the sign indicating that I had just crested Donahue Pass it surprised me. Maybe this would be easier than I was expecting.

On the south side of Donahue Pass I caught an elderly gentleman with an enormous camera slung around his neck. He had a patch of unkempt silver hair and distant look that reminded me of a college science professor.

"Hello! You're moving fast! Are you doing the whole trail?" he asked.

"Hi! I'm headed to Whitney. What about you?" I replied with a smile, the ritualistic exchange coming as a welcome change-up.

"Me too, me too. But slowly. I did the whole thing a few years ago and really pushed myself, but I decided to come back and take my time so I could get some great pictures," he said, shaking his beast of a camera.

We chatted for a couple minutes, and as I left him to his photo ops I was struck by the fact that everyone on this trail was achieving the same thing, but in very different ways and for different reasons. Ego, connection to the natural world, escape, fitness, hobbies, or desire to quench an unquenchable thirst — the JMT meant something else to all of us. In that moment I felt both separate from and yet connected to them all.

I passed Thousand Island Lake and was struck by its size and raw beauty. I thought of my usual backpacking crew (my dad, uncle, and cousins) and vowed to bring them back to this place. Earlier in the day this train of thought would have given me a pang of sadness, but now it was all hope and appreciation. I had managed to shift my energy to a more productive place. I would no doubt need to harness that skill on multiple occasions during this trip, and it was encouraging to notice that I had already been successful once.

I crested a rise and then found myself flanking a small lake, tip-toeing billy-goat style just inches from the water. At the end of the lake a sturdy, wood bridge straddled the slowly trickling outlet. I crossed the bridge and attacked the steep downhill ravine on the other side without a second thought. It wasn't only steep, it was downright treacherous; a couple times I had to lower myself down with my hands. Odd that the John Muir Trail would devolve into this questionable alleyway. In hindsight I should have paid attention to the "wrongness" I was beginning to feel, but at the time I waved it away and kept forging ahead.

At the bottom of the crevice I was met with a road junction; three different paths going three different directions, with no signage anywhere. Up to this point the trail had been exceedingly well marked and I'd been able to navigate without even paying attention. Now I was in a bit of a pickle. I had the brief thought that perhaps the trail had actually kept going straight and that I wasn't supposed to have crossed the bridge. But I didn't remember seeing any other trail options, and I had no desire to climb back up the cliff I had just descended. I took out my maps and studied them carefully. I knew the general direction I had to go, but I couldn't tell exactly where I was. I stood there chewing on my lip, staring at each trail, trying to will my accumulated knowledge and intuition into giving me a definitive answer. Nothing. Like so much in life, I would have to make the best choice possible and deal with the consequences as they appeared. I took a deep breath, set my thumbs under the shoulder straps of my pack, and chose the trail that seemed slightly larger and more traveled.

Another mile of steep downhill and I was almost fully convinced that I had lost the John Muir Trail. There was a sheer cliff to my left, cut by the thundering rapid 100 feet below. To my right the mountain side rose almost as steeply, disappearing into the horizon. The trail I was following could barely be called that word. It was more like a game path since it gradually became smaller and was covered in brush. When I walked face-first into a well-spun spider web, the sinking feeling in my stomach hit bottom. Breaking gossamer on a trail generally only happens in the early morning as it means you are the first person of the day to pass through. It was early afternoon and the John Muir Trail is one of the most heavily traveled corridors in the Sierras. This was not the JMT.

Fear and frustration were quickly rising inside me. Being lost in the wilderness evokes a primitive terror not unlike the previously mentioned fear of being eaten alive. Will I starve? Will I die alone? Will I be remembered? You don't actually think these things will happen, but that little boy (or girl) hiding in all of us still has a voice. I've heard this voice many times, and know in my bones how debilitating it can be to listen to it and let it take hold. I've found that logic and action are my best weapons in these situations, so I kept moving and reviewed my options.

1) I could backtrack and try to find where I'd lost the trail, losing hours and precious energy.
2) I could stay put and hope a mythical fairy creature would come to my rescue.
3) I could keep moving forward and try to reconnect with the trail at some point.

I really, really didn't want to backtrack. Not only would it be significant uphill, there is something monumentally distasteful about losing ground. I never really considered this as an option. The mythical fairy creature idea had some merit and would certainly make for a good story, but it didn't seem prudent to rely on the whims of the fantastical. This meant I would keep heading down and hope to eventually get back to the JMT.

I kept trudging ahead, and abruptly the small path I was navigating intersected a wide thoroughfare. The cliff and trees on my right had receded, and hope shot through me as I was touched by real sunlight for first time in hours. I studied my maps again and determined that I had just found the Pacific Crest Trail. Hallelujah. While not the JMT, the PCT was the next best thing. One of the most storied and famous trails in history, the PCT runs 2,650 miles from Mexico to Canada and parallels the entire JMT (in fact in many cases they are the same trail). In this case they were separate trails but if I followed the PCT it appeared I would be able to start walking in John Muir's footsteps once again near Reds Meadow some five miles from here.

My pace had slowed while lost, as if I wasn't fully committed to the direction I was headed, but now that I knew where I was going I attacked the trail with renewed vigor. I was still frustrated by the lost time and energy (in looking at the map it appeared I added quite a few miles to an already long day) and channeled that anger into my legs. The area I was now hiking in had been ravaged by a wildfire in the recent past, and it was desolate and ugly, with only blackened shards of trees to break the monotony. With no view and a quickly waning sun, I just put my head down and moved.

At some point I saw people up ahead, hiking perpendicular to me. Another trail? Then I saw the sign for the John Muir Trail and silently rejoiced, sending a hearty thank you to whatever cosmic powers had intervened on my behalf. There was a large log at the trail junction, and I decided to celebrate by taking off my pack and sitting for a minute. Just as I sat down, the hikers I had seen ambled up. Two athletic, middle-aged women with gigantic packs and tired smiles. They were planning to complete the trail in three weeks and would be stopping for the evening in Reds Meadow where they would buy dinner and feast. Spending time with people and eating real food sounded amazing, but it didn't jive with my timeline and was ultimately not what I was out here to do. This would be the first of many encounters where I was presented with a choice that sounded infinitely better than what I had planned, but I felt a quiet pride each time I was able to take the long-view and not succumb to transitory pleasures.

The sky was darkening quickly so I kept moving. It was clear that I wouldn't hit my 39-mile goal for the day, so I vowed to hike until sunset. Stopping only briefly to take a picture of some otherworldly rock formations on the outskirts of Devils Postpile National Monument, I made good time and found myself climbing switchbacks out of the valley as the sun began to dip below the ridge behind me.

The side of a mountain is never an ideal place to camp because level ground is scarce, but it was my only option at this point. I hiked for 15 minutes as the dark continued to descend around me, eyes peeled for the scarcest hint of flat ground. Finally I spotted a small patch of almost-level earth under a large tree, and decided it would have to do.

I began my evening routine with haste, and let my mind and body relax into the practiced movements of camp life. Suddenly a sharp crack broke the silence, and I jumped as if I'd been shot! I twirled around and stared awestruck at two enormous bucks locking horns 20 feet away. Two regal animals, crashing into each other, with steam rising from their nostrils and dust swirling around their hooves ... it was a spectacle to behold. I shook my head in amazement as I watched them, both because it was epic and because I couldn't believe they let me witness it. After a demanding day, this was a profound reminder of why I was here and what I hoped to gain from this experience. Even if I felt alone, I wasn't — and there is a gift in every moment.

Chapter 8
Faith and Pragmatism

*(Day 3 - Red Cones to somewhere below
Bear Ridge, 27 miles)*

"Today I have grown taller from walking with the trees."
— Karle Wilson Baker

After another long night contorting my body into strange shapes to avoid the lantern moon, I was more than ready to emerge from my tent when my alarm went off. I quickly downed some breakfast and then set about the now familiar routine of stuffing my gear into my pack. "Carefully placing" is actually much more accurate, as every item had a specific home that was born by logic and utility. I would start the day wearing most or all of my clothing for warmth, but then as I removed layers they would become soft barriers between my bear canister and my back. Most of my food was kept in a stuff sack, however my snacks for the day were in easy-access pouches that zipped along my waist belt. Water was in a reservoir (with a hose that I clipped to my shoulder strap) that slipped into a vertical sleeve in the pack, as well as a backup bottle secured by mesh webbing on the left, bottom panel. Sleep items were stored in the main pack compartment, and other things that I may need quick access to in the smaller upper pouch (toilet paper, first aid kit, etc.) or back-mesh webbing (maps).

A Lost Era

When I first started backpacking as a kid in the '80's we would dangle stainless-steel sierra cups from our packs and slake our thirst from rivers and lakes as we passed by. There is nothing in the world more refreshing than glacial water that has just melted or sprung from the earth. Unfortunately those days are long gone as livestock has become more prevalent in wilderness areas and water-borne illness is common (particularly Giardia – a parasite that causes very serious GI issues for up to six weeks). While it is still probably safe to drink water directly from a spring, all other water sources are potentially contaminated and should be treated before consumption. Filters, tablets, purifiers, UV light – there are many different ways to make water safe, and there continue to be lighter and faster options available.

What I used on this trip was a 3.6 oz SteriPen that takes 90 seconds to kill 99.99 percent of bacteria, viruses, and protozoa with UV light. For the last decade I have been filtering my water with relatively heavy and cumbersome equipment, and the SteriPen marks a significant improvement in weight, ease, and speed. The only downside to using a UV system like the SteriPen is that no filter is included, so you must find water that is already fairly clean or you will be drinking dirt. On the JMT that wasn't an issue, and even if it had been I was prepared to channel my inner MacGyver and use my shirt as a makeshift filter. The need to problem-solve and make do with the tools at hand is part of the fun of the backcountry!

There is something inherently calming about finding a spot in the woods, borrowing it for an evening, and then moving on with no trace left behind. It evokes a sense of oneness and acceptance; a feeling that all things are as they should be. I was lost in this place as I loaded my pack, enjoying the satisfaction of perfectly placed puzzle pieces.

I gave one last look around my campsite to make sure I hadn't missed anything, and then headed to a nearby rivulet to fill up my water bottle. Before I had taken two steps, I was startled out of my reverie by a high-pitched yipping bark. Not 10 feet away was a lanky coyote standing on a downed tree as if he was Simba, chest tall and head thrown back. He was looking at me without looking at me, as only canines can. I took a deep breath to let my now speeding heart rate drop, and then began walking again. Another bark stopped me in my tracks, and while I don't speak fluent coyote I swear it was a warning. But what danger was he signaling? A bear? Bad water? Or perhaps he was just letting me know the stream belonged to him? Regardless, I decided it was prudent to acquiesce to his superior instincts and left the stream behind. I could get water further up the trail.

I had to hike cross-country for a few minutes to find the trail, and when I got there I stopped to adjust straps on my pack and secure my water bottle. As I turned to put my pack back on I was again surprised by the coyote. This time the scraggly creature was still and silent, standing on a boulder above me. I wasn't exactly scared, but his behavior was odd and unnerving. With tingling skin and the hair on the back of my neck standing straight, I vacated the area with haste.

As I climbed the long switchbacks out of the valley, I could hear the coyote somewhere below me. He varied between the yipping I'd already heard and the forlorn, eerie howl we all associate with wild dogs. His song continued to become quieter and more distant, and just before I reached the spine of the mountain I heard an answering cry. And then silence. Maybe he was just looking for a friend.

The uphill start to the day had rapidly opened up my legs and lungs, and I fell into a solid pace, alternating between jogging and fast hiking. Aware that I still needed to get water, I kept scanning the terrain around me for patches of fertility, and tuned my ears to the telltale trickle of a trailside stream. So far all was dry, and I was getting thirsty. This was yet another opportunity to recognize stress, manage it, and practice critical thinking in spite of it. I took out my map and looked for the squiggly blue line that would bisect the trail soonest. It was hard to tell, but it appeared that I would be crossing a river within the next couple miles.

Within what seemed like minutes the trail dipped and I heard the soft rush of water. Thirst spiking, I quickened my pace for the last hundred yards and had my water bottle and SteriPen in hand as I reached the river. As I swirled the UV pen in the container, a burly man walked over from a small tent on the other side of the river.

"Are you the guy hiking 40 miles a day?" he asked through a lumberjack beard.

"Uh … I'm trying to go that fast. How do you know who I am?" I stammered in bewilderment. Was I somehow famous?

Laughing, he said, "I stopped in Reds Meadow for dinner last night and talked to some women who told me about you. Then I must have hiked past your camp in the dark. That's a blistering pace, man. How's it going so far?"

"Of course," I thought, "those women I met at the PCT/JMT junction had mentioned me over dinner." Swapping stories about other hikers is another common element of through-hiking etiquette. Just as strangers at a party will unconsciously begin discussing sports or children to find shared ground, long-distance backpackers almost always ask about each other.

"I feel good so far. There is only so much daylight, but I'm going to keep moving as fast as I can. Have a good trip," I replied.

I offered a brief wave, tucked my water bottle back into its pouch, crossed the river, and continued on my way. As I began to climb up once more, I realized I hadn't even asked the big man about his trip. Bad form, but I was antsy to put the miles behind me. His question about my daily mileage goal had shined a spotlight on the fact that I wasn't quite on pace. "Better put the hammer down today," I thought.

I continued the gradual climb throughout the morning and at some point began floating in the warm waters of my alpha brainwave state just as I had the day before.

"Put that in your pipe and smoke it"

We like to see things as mystical and transcendent (I certainly do), but there is simple physiology at work behind "The Zone". Alpha brainwaves occur at times of extreme relaxation and meditation, and spontaneous creativity, increased memory, and an overall feeling of peace and harmony characterize this state. I first discovered this euphoric Neverland while trail running, and now I crave it and search for it. There are measurable hormonal responses to brainwave states, so when you hear someone say they are addicted to running they very well could be.

I saw a road sign for Purple Lake and Cascade Valley, and smiled at the memory of my first trip to this range 27 years previously; Cascade is where it all began. The JMT wouldn't take me down into the heart of the valley, but I would pass close enough to feel its pull. As I walked the world around me flickered with fleeting images, and for a time I was two people in two places. Eventually I passed the turnoff to Cascade Valley and gave a brief nod of thanks — who would I be without this place?

Abruptly the slope steepened noticeably and the foliage began to thin. Having already reviewed my map I knew I must be starting the final push toward Silver Pass. I could just see the outline of a hiker in the distance, and I decided to make a game of catching him or her. It's funny how the Universe will humble those who need it, and for me it always seems to happen instantly. I remember once while struggling to put together a monstrous piece of gym equipment, I finally managed to snap the last piece into place. As I stood up, dancing wildly and exclaiming "I am the shit!" I gave myself a concussion on the machine's steel crossbeam. To this day my wife will laugh uncontrollably if reminded of this story. I actually laugh too. It's a fantastic parable, and I try to remember its message as I live my life: **There is a fine line between confidence and cockiness.** Belief in yourself is great; as long as you don't fall into the trap of thinking you have it all figured out.

I did finally catch the hiker just below Silver Pass, but it took me much longer than I thought it would and my lungs were on fire. At 10,735 feet above sea level I had conquered the slightly higher Donahue Pass yesterday with much less effort, but this was exceedingly difficult. The negative effects of extreme altitude are funny in that they generally take a couple days to fully present themselves. Days two or three are usually the worst, and then oxygen-carrying capacity gradually improves until you are fully acclimated after 10-14 days.

The "hiker" actually turned out to be two backpackers toting traditional internal frame packs that were bursting at the seams.

They engaged me with warm smiles, and the relaxed nonchalance that manifests after extended time in the backcountry. Rangy and tanned, they were almost halfway into a month-long JMT trek that centered on trout fishing and whiskey. Yes, we were all here for different reasons. The idea of trying to get to the top of Silver Pass after taking a swig of Jim Beam literally made me queasy. (Of course I always have that reaction when thinking about hard alcohol — my bachelor party in 2008 was a little too memorable.) While the thought of alcohol made me shiver, fresh trout sounded downright orgasmic. They had caught six fish the day before and had them for dinner and breakfast. I eyed their fishing poles longingly, wished them well, and then resumed my journey.

After the gut punch of Silver Pass I was rewarded with a nice 10-mile downhill section. My heart rate dropped and I added some running to the mix, but I clearly wasn't going to reach 40 miles this day. Like the day before, I decided I'd simply hike until dark and then find a place to stop for the night. Even though I was fully aware that I was going to fall short of my mileage goal for the second straight day, I wasn't yet giving it any mental or emotional energy. If I had let myself think about it more it would have been clear that making up those lost miles would be next to impossible, but at this moment in time I was immersed completely in the belief that everything would work out as it should. This is a dance I often engage in, and I'm still figuring out the steps. In endurance sports, there is a balance between faith and pragmatism. You need a large and balanced measure of both in order to be effective, but too much of either can be catastrophic.

As dusk started to descend my slowing footfalls brought me to the base of Bear Ridge. I was tired and it was almost dark, but I still had something to give. I began trudging up the steep switchbacks, taking solace in the fact that every step earned tonight would be behind me in the morning. The night before I camped on a hillside, but this was much steeper. I squinted into the growing blackness, trying to find flat ground anywhere. Nothing. Higher and higher I climbed, but all I saw were boulders and trees jutting from the near-vertical earth.

Eventually I got out my headlamp and continued my search using its diffused light. I finally spotted a small patch of bare ground just off the trail. It wasn't level, but it was the best option I'd seen since beginning my ascent almost an hour before. Exhausted, I set up my tarp and climbed under my quilt in record time. The slope was steep enough that throughout the night I kept sliding off my sleeping pad until my feet stretched the limits of the tarp netting. I would briefly wake and caterpillar back up, and then fall asleep once more. Despite this, I managed to get my best night of sleep yet.

Something I haven't mentioned yet is that I was carrying a GPS receiver that allowed me to send pre-set messages to loved ones, and for them to track my progress. It also included an SOS button that would send an emergency message and transmit my location if I found myself in trouble. It was the first time in my adventurous lifetime I'd ever carried something like this, but it made sense. It also made my wife and mom much more comfortable with the idea of me spending multiple days alone in the wilderness.

I had agreed to send an "I'm OK" message every night when I stopped for the evening, and I dutifully complied. It actually gave me something to look forward to, because even though I couldn't see them or hear their voices, it was comforting to reach out and touch my family in some small way. I would imagine my wife smiling as she got my message for the evening and then posting an update on Facebook, and it made me feel less alone.

When I returned home I learned that the message I sent on this hill below Bear Ridge never went through. Apparently everyone was silently terrified but refused to reach out to each other because they were trying to be positive and didn't want to add more stress to an already-stressful situation. My next message went through fine, but knowing that I caused that kind of heartache still hurts to this day. It was a sobering reminder that as independent as I like to think I am, my decisions affect other people.

Chapter 9
In the Groove

(Day 4 - Somewhere below Bear Ridge to McClure Meadow, 27 miles)

*"The biggest human temptation
is to settle for too little."*
— Thomas Merton

I awoke at dawn surprisingly refreshed. My body seemed to be adapting to the elevation and long nights spent tightly curled on uneven ground. In a grateful and contented headspace, I savored the morning routine slightly longer than usual. Rather than making a beeline for my bear canister to hurriedly shovel fuel into my engine, I stretched for a few minutes and took in my surroundings. Then I recorded a short video journal entry and began to gather my things. (In reviewing the video footage after my trip I noticed that I started to look like a mountain man at this point in the trip. The beard was a pretty good look, but the altitude made my face look puffy and foreign.)

Like the morning before, I was completely out of water after downing my breakfast SPIZ.

SPIZ ... Really?

Yes, you read that right — and I assure you I have heard every joke you can come up with. Despite the name SPIZ is a fantastic fuel source for ultra-endurance athletes as it is basically a complete meal in powdered form; each serving has over 500 calories and a healthy dose of macro and micro nutrients. I used SPIZ for my first Ironman as well as this John Muir trip, and it served me excellently both times.

I remembered seeing a small waterfall two switchbacks behind me, and while I didn't relish the thought of back-tracking even a single step, it felt sensible to fill up with water while I could. When I reached the waterfall I realized it was further off the trail — and steeper — than I thought. I clambered down the loose dirt and bounced from boulder to boulder like a mountain pinball until I reached the pool.

As I caught my breath and collected water, I reflected on the downhill strategy I had just employed and how much more comfortable I had become in situations like these. Hurtling downward evokes an exhilarating terror, and the key to success and safety is to trust your body. Most rookie runners instinctively try to fight and control the momentum by braking themselves, however this slows you down and uses infinitely more muscular energy. Instead it is faster, more efficient, and more fun to let gravity pull you and to focus on foot turnover and placement, engaging core muscles, and looking a few seconds ahead to plan your route.

Hydration taken care of, I scrambled back up to the trail on all fours and turned south once more. I was definitely more acclimated this morning, and I made short work of the remainder of the switchbacks up to Bear Ridge. On the ridge, the path leveled out, and I was able to fall into a steady jog. It remained uncomfortable and tiring to run for any length of time, so I speed walked (a manly, backpacker's speed walk with no arm flailing) and caught my breath every few minutes. It was fun to move fast, particularly at the beginning of the day. I have always been a morning person. Something about the fresh start and infinite possibilities of the day to come just quickens my pulse. On the JMT that mindset manifested into a feeling of exuberant confidence that made anything seem achievable.

My mood was also lightened by the knowledge that I would be picking up my resupply at the Muir Trail Ranch in a few hours. That meant people to talk to, a semblance of civilization, and the emotional charge of hitting my halfway point. It also meant a whole bag of Snickers. I am a nutritionist by trade and my diet reflects this. I can enjoy a bowl of Cap'n Crunch as much or more than the next guy, but over the years I have changed my emotional and physical relationship to food so that I crave real things that support my health and my goals. I think sometimes people wonder how and why I deprive myself, but the reality is that I love food and never feel like I'm missing out. A big salad chockfull of veggies, nuts, berries, avocado, and grass-fed steak or wild salmon is infinitely more satisfying to me than lasagna or a hot fudge sundae. With that said, I couldn't wait to tear open that bag of Snickers.

After Bear Ridge, the morning was spent gradually climbing once again. I had left the burnt and scarred ugliness far behind by this point, and every bend in the trail revealed vistas, meadows, and jagged edges that can only be properly captured by the mind. Every picture I took failed to fully depict the scale and raw imminence of the Sierra-Nevada landscape. I take very few snapshots when I'm on walkabout — mostly this has to do with my preference for living in the moment rather than attempting to record the moment, but the other reason is simply that pictures almost always fail to bring the mountains to life.

Food: Friend or Enemy?

This could obviously be a book of its own (and has been), but my editor wouldn't let me get away with saying that I've changed my relationship with food without explaining myself! It has been a lifelong journey and has encompassed many things; having patience with the process, paying attention to how I feel after consuming inadequate fuel, appreciating how I look and perform when I eat in a manner that supports my goals, and remembering that I don't have to be perfect to make progress. If you are trying to lose weight, eat more healthfully, or simply gain more control of your diet, try this easy but powerful two-step combo:

- Clearly define your goals. Write them down, put pictures up, etc. Cliché but true — if you don't know where you're going and why, you will never get there. People without clear goals and energy behind them are the ones who binge on the weekends and tell themselves that the magic will happen on Monday.

- Take a second before you eat and ask yourself, "Why am I eating this? Am I hungry? Tired? Bored? Sad?" There are countless reasons that we are motivated to eat, and fueling our bodies is only one (and not the most common). The answers to your question may surprise you, and the process will empower you. What you ultimately decide to do with the new information is up to you, but at least you've established control over your food decisions rather than continue to let your food control you.

I passed Marie Lake and finally made my way to Selden Pass. At virtually the same elevation as Silver Pass the day before, cresting Selden felt much easier. Acclimation is a wonderful thing. When a trained athlete first begins exercising at altitude it can be very frustrating, because you are used to a certain fluidity, competence, and strength that can be severely limited by lack of oxygen. It's like trying to box with one hand tied behind your back. The flipside is how awesome it feels to have that hand untied.

Once I planted my feet atop Selden Pass, I wouldn't have to go up again for hours as I had almost exactly 3,000 feet of elevation to lose before strolling through the gate at Muir Trail Ranch in the valley far below. I briefly looked behind me and down at the valley I had just climbed out of and shook my head slightly. The plight of one small soul against the backdrop of such an infinite and unforgiving wilderness never ceases to thrill and amaze me. Enchanted by the moment, I began racing down the other side of the pass. Every third or fourth switchback was so precipitous that even my finely-tuned downhill strategy wasn't effective — there was simply more velocity than my legs were capable of keeping up with. Making small zigzags can help arrest momentum without wasting energy, so I added this to my routine. As the terrain varied I sprinted, shambled, trotted, and zigzagged my way down.

Going downhill offers such a stark contrast to the slow uphill trudge that I often find myself greatly overestimating my speed. As I "flew" down the mountain I kept expecting to see signs for the turnoff to Muir Trail Ranch. When the mid-day sun began to bake me with no sign of reprieve, I felt like I was trapped in some *Twilight Zone* downhill purgatory. It's funny how the mind plays tricks on you when you're in the middle of nowhere and haven't spoken to anyone for days on end. Did I miss a turnoff somehow? Was I damned to keep running downhill for eternity or at least until I reached the gates of Hell? I wondered if Satan would be hoarding my Snickers and if I could somehow convince him to share. I knew I was slightly delirious from spending so much time in my own head, but I was okay with it. As long as I entertained and amused myself, I didn't see any harm in it. In fact, I've had some of my best ideas in this state, allowing my mind to create without constraint or judgment.

I eventually saw the side trail to Muir Trail Ranch and skidded to stop with a burst of excitement. I made the quick right turn and decided to walk the last two miles to the ranch as my legs were beat from hours of jarring and pounding. Once again I overestimated my pace, and just as I was about to pull out my map for a progress check I saw a wooden gate in the distance.

Muir Trail Ranch was charming and quaint, with a main cabin, three or four log outbuildings, and a small horse stable. As I walked up I saw no sign of life. The only thing moving was a small, wooden "Muir Trail Ranch" sign listlessly swinging in the breeze. This was a little too reminiscent a western ghost town, and I certainly wasn't John Wayne with a buffet waiting just off the movie set. I knew the ranch was set to close for the season two days from now, and I had to actively shut the flood gates to stop the rising tide of my anxiety. Did they close early?

Just as my brain was about to shift into overdrive to figure out how to proceed, I heard voices from behind one of the buildings. Then I saw a bell and handwritten sign that said, "Please ring for help." With a sigh of relief I pulled on the bell rope and removed my pack. And waited … and waited.

Frowning, I turned to go find the voices and then heard a door creak. Standing in the front door of the main cabin was perhaps the oldest woman I'd ever seen. She was short and sturdy, with wispy white hair and steel in her eyes. She nodded curtly and began to shuffle toward me using a walking stick for support. (Shuffle is actually a generous term — she covered the 50 feet between us in what seemed like 10 minutes.) As I waited for her to arrive, I laughed to myself. I had just covered over 100 miles through the wild, moving as fast as I could, and now I could do nothing but be patient. Even though I had been trying to appreciate the entire experience and to let it all in, this was a good reminder to stop and smell the roses.

We are Human BEINGS

This was a good reminder for life back in the real world as well. I think many of us are good at pursuing our passions and engaging with life — particularly if we were raised by baby boomers who may have seen drawbacks in their parent's mindset. This approach to life can be a double-edged sword. Running fast, creating, learning, and exploring are fun, but I don't want my achievements to define me. When I am capable of fulfillment by "being" rather than "doing," I may just be ready to earn my black belt in life. Well that, and washing my dishes in a timely manner.

The mountain gnome disguised as an old woman eventually made her way to me, and then we slowly walked together toward a shed to my left after I informed her why I had come. When we finally turned the corner, I was immediately struck with sensory overload. Scores of multicolored buckets were stacked on top of one another beneath a sign indicating that the food and supplies they contained were up for grabs. Apparently this was the infamous "bucket graveyard" I had read about. All year backpackers had resupplied here, leaving their remnants behind. Perhaps they had overestimated their needs or weren't as hungry as expected. Or maybe during the first part of their trip they lost the taste for something they packed in their resupply bucket and decided to simply leave it at the Ranch (this actually happened to me with some energy bars). Whatever the reason, there had to be 500 pounds of food sitting in front of me, just waiting to be claimed. I let my widened eyes relax and shook off my momentary stupor. There would be time enough to look through these buckets if

I wanted to. First things first.

As the wizened ranch owner rooted around the shed for the bucket with my name on it, I looked around. There was an open picnic area next to the shed, and a woman had her pack propped on a table and was rummaging through it with her back to me.

"Hello!" I said cheerfully, happy to finally be here.

She turned with a smile and nodded, still focused on her task.

The old woman had located my bucket and called me over. Sure enough, there it sat in all of its orange Home Depot splendor. I have to say it was a little surreal to see this lonely bucket, two months and 250 miles later. Particularly because it contained my lifeblood. In that moment, this bucket was more important to me than anything else in the world.

I carried it over to a picnic table and took out my pocketknife to cut through the prodigious packing tape.

"How long have you been out?" asked the woman who I had briefly greeted a few minutes before.

She had finished sorting through her pack and was sitting on a bench munching on a bar.

"Just a couple days. I started at Tuolumne on Monday morning. You?" I replied.

Her eyebrows raised and she said, "You're covering some ground. I'm doing the trail in 15 days, and I thought that was fast!"

I finally got my bucket open and poured its contents onto the table so I could take inventory. Mostly it was a duplicate of everything I had been surviving on for the last two days, however there were some tantalizing additions I had forgotten about: Gluten-free cookies (I know, I'm weird — but I can't help it if my body doesn't like gluten), Justin's peanut-butter cups, Zico coconut water, and of course the bag of Snickers. An interesting phenomenon happens in the back-country — the alchemy of hunger and deprivation turns food into gold — all food. So being presented with good food is like going to Disneyland on ecstasy. I downed a coconut water and reveled in its cool sweetness. Then I opened a Snickers, took a second to appreciate the weight and texture, deeply inhaled the chocolate scent, and proceeded to inhale it. I probably looked like my dog, spastically horking down his food as if it will be stolen at any moment.

As I ate and relaxed, I chatted with the woman on the bench. She was an Ironman triathlete and Air Force Reservist, and had decided to hike the JMT in between military assignments. We had much in common, and it was pleasant to connect over something other than this trail that had been consuming all of my energy and thought over the last three days.

Presently, a group of three backpackers wandered into the picnic area. They looked like an odd bunch and talking to them quickly proved my instincts correct. A couple in their 70's and their son who was about my age, they had hiked the entire Pacific Crest Trail twice and were completing the JMT for their third time. That is significant time away from civilization, and it made them a little rough around the edges. Perhaps it's impossible to spend that much time in the wild without it getting into your blood. The father in particular seemed slightly more wolf than man. They were nice enough, but I found myself relieved that we wouldn't be spending more time together.

Before reloading my bear can I decided to peruse the bucket buffet. I was aware of a growing craving for salt, particularly in light of the sweet treats I had just sucked down. Apparently I wasn't the only one. I looked through bucket after bucket for something salty (Fritos sounded exquisite), but couldn't find anything. Disappointed, I made a mental note to pack more salty foods the next time I did something like this.

Refreshed but acutely aware of the sun's low position in the sky, I shifted into work mode and began preparing my pack for departure.

"You're not going to check out the hot springs?" asked the reservist, seeming surprised that I was packing up.

"What hot springs?" I replied with a frown.

I am obsessed with hot water and will go in a hot tub any chance I get; particularly if I've been cold for any length of time or if my body is sore. Check, check — I did not need this distraction.

"Blayney hot springs. It's just down the road and supposed to be incredible. I planned a full day here because I didn't want to miss it."

I let myself think about it for less than two seconds. Good God would that be nice. But no time. And, like the dinner invitation at Red's Meadow, it's not what I was here for.

"No hot springs for me. I have to keep moving. Have fun!"

I gave her a wave, nodded to the strange, feral family, and made my boots move toward the front gate of the ranch.

That was an incredibly difficult moment for me. All day I had been looking forward to the excitement of food, people, and a break in the routine. Now I was leaving all that behind and would immediately have to hike straight up and out of the valley. Being in touch with my goals is the only thing that allowed me to overcome the inertia of sitting on that picnic bench. I still remember Newton's first law from high school physics: An object in motion will stay in motion and an object at rest will stay at rest unless acted upon by an outside force. That outside force was my will driven by purpose.

Belly and pack full, I felt like a swollen flea as I trudged up the trail. Even so, being on the back half of my trip was rewarding, and it felt good to move again. As I walked, I reviewed my maps and formulated a plan for the remainder of the day. I would be gradually climbing up to Muir Pass for the next 20 miles, but I clearly wouldn't make it there before running out of daylight. The good news was that the trail appeared to be lined with meadows for much of the way, and I relished the idea of camping somewhere relatively flat and spacious after the previous two nights spent balanced on hillsides. Content with my plan, I locked into a solid pace and found my rhythm for the first time that day.

At some point minutes or hours later, I found myself facing a rushing river. I could see the trail continuing up the valley on the other side, but there was 30 feet of icy, fast-flowing water in-between.

"We're going to have to cross it," said a pleasant, female voice.

I jumped slightly and turned around. Sitting on a rock just off the trail was a plump Asian woman with a kind face. I had been so focused on the river I hadn't even noticed her as I passed by.

"I have a JMT app on my iPhone, and it says this is the only way across for miles. If we take our shoes off it shouldn't be that big of a deal. It's not that deep," she said, holding up her iPhone.

iPhone? We're in the woods! A little bewildered, I studied the rest of the scene. Her enormous pack was sitting next to her with gadgets sticking out in all directions. In fact the entire back of her pack was covered with a solar panel for charging her electronics. This was definitely a unique way to "rough it".

I sat down on another rock close by, and we talked as we removed our shoes. She was a pharmacist from San Francisco and had a month off in-between jobs. Not wanting to sit around and waste time, she decided to hike the JMT. Her husband thought she was crazy, but that just made her want to do it more. She'd never done anything like this before and wasn't in particularly good shape, but she figured if she planned well and moved slowly enough she could complete the trail in under a month. I couldn't decide if I was impressed, annoyed, or amused. Regardless of how I felt about her decision to brave the trail, she won me over with her sweet absurdity and irreverent joy.

The river was cold, but actually refreshed my feet after a long day. The hardest things about crossing a river are avoiding sharp rocks and not falling in. Swiftly moving water generally looks innocuous — until you step into it. Still, I made it to the other side without incident.

As we dried our feet and put our boots back on, the pharmacist invited me to dinner. Apparently her iPhone told her that there would be a great campsite just ahead, and she was planning to camp there and make spaghetti. I politely declined as I still wanted to hike for at least another hour, but I had another brief pang of regret. Spaghetti sounded amazing, and who knew what other treasures were hiding in her leprechaun pack. Maybe she'd pull out a bottle of wine or a satellite phone so I could call Jen.

"You're not here for a pasta feed or to make friends with eccentric drug pushers. You're here to see what you're capable of," I told myself. And with that, I kicked into high gear and left her fiddling with her phone.

The trail mostly leveled off after the river, and while there was a minor uphill gradient it felt flat compared to what my legs were used to. I enjoyed the meadow scenery to my right and smiled at the sounds of dusk in the wild. I thought about how hard it is to leave people behind and face the unknown alone, but how the very act of doing so instills great strength. I realized as I mentally explored this that the hardest part of being alone isn't the loneliness, but the fact that there is nothing to distract your brain. You have to be mentally on point at all times. In many ways it reminded me of Ironman — except this was a week-long Ironman broken up by cold, uncomfortable sleep.

As the sun was setting I spotted a picturesque campsite just off the trail. It was flat and surrounded by a river on two sides. (It also had places to sit and cook, which the backpacker in me instinctively looked for even though I wouldn't need them this night). I set up my tarp tent and reveled in the fact that I could fully stretch the guy lines and that no part of it was pressed up against rocks or hanging off a cliff.

Before retiring for the evening I braved the cold to sit on a large, flat boulder by the river. I thought about the day and the trip so far. I was proud of myself for showing steadfast commitment to my vision and for the progress I'd made, both physically and mentally. With one last look at the moonlight on the water, I couldn't help but smile at my overall impression of the journey up to this point. I made my way to bed, and as I climbed underneath my quilt, shivering slightly from the chill, I wondered what was in store for me tomorrow. If I had known the answer, I'm not sure I would have been able to sleep.

Day 1 - Ready to hit the trail

LITTLE YOSEMITE CAMPGROUND	4.3	6.9
GLACIER POINT	8.2	11.3
HALF DOME	8.2	11.3
CLOUDS REST	10.5	17.0
MERCED LAKE	13.1	21.0
TENAYA LAKE	16.4	26.0
TUOLUMNE MEADOWS	27.3	44.0
MOUNT WHITNEY VIA JOHN MUIR TRAIL	211.0	340.0

NO PETS ON TRAILS

First trail sign - 211 miles to Whitney

Sunrise with Half Dome in the distance

Nevada Falls - a dry year

Somewhere near Sunrise Camp

Wild horses in Lyell Canyon

My empty food sack with the bottom cut out

Bear aftermath - he actually unwrapped a few things very daintily

Demian trying to cheer me up with some oatmeal

2nd Attempt - An early start

Dawn on the Tuolumne River

Morning mist rising from the Lyell Fork

Nameless lake below Donahue Pass

Looking down on Thousand Island Lake

Strange rock formations on the outskirts of Devil's Postpile

Turns out I slept with a deer herd on Day 2

Purple Lake

Cascade Valley

The rear-view from Silver Pass

First signs of fall

Hillside campsite below Bear Ridge

Muir Trail Ranch

The barren path to Muir Pass

Muir Hut

Walking into the Range of Light

Upper Palisade Lake

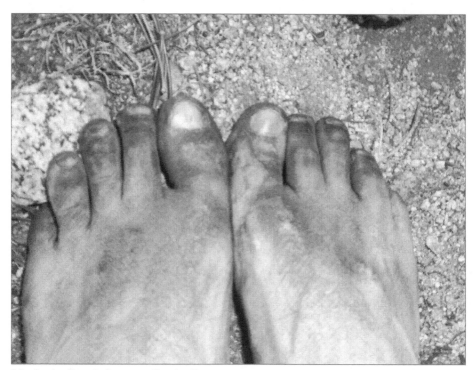

My feet after 4 days on the trail

Lake Marjorie

A pool of snowmelt below Pinchot Pass

Crossing the bridge on the way to Rae Lakes

Lower Rae Lake

Moon rising over Upper Rae Lake

Looking back on my way to Glen Pass

Scanning the horizon after coming down from Forester Pass

Crabtree Ranger Station - my camping spot for the last night

A snowy morning - almost there

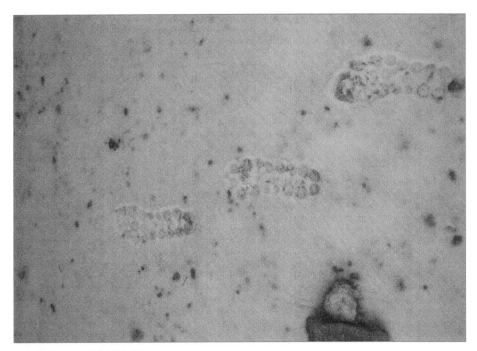

Footprints marking the way

Snow dusted rock surrounding Timberline Lake

On the climb to Whitney - my traveled path extends past the horizon

View from the top of Whitney

Scruffy selfie on top of Whitney

Chapter 10
Melting Down

(Day 5 — McClure Meadow to Palisade Lakes, 28 miles)

"Whether you think you can or think you can't — you're right."
— Henry Ford

It was cold. I could feel it leeching into me through my quilt and beanie. I blinked groggily in the blackness and decided that moving was the only way to get warmer. If nothing else it would keep my mind off the aching chill. I sat up, my lower half still covered by the failing quilt, head just grazing the top of my tarp, and quickly gathered and packed everything I could reach; it had taken me only a day on the trail to realize that this practice would keep me warmer for a few more minutes every morning.

When I had accomplished everything I could from this sitting position, I forced myself up and finished breaking down camp. I distinctly remember the feeling I had that frosty morning — every fiber of my being telling me to huddle under my quilt and wait for a magical rescue chopper. I remember it so clearly because I've experienced it countless times before. Toeing the freezing Pacific water seconds before a triathlon starts; looking with wide eyes at the landscape 10,000 feet below while waiting for the "Go!" to jump from an airplane; dragging slowly down the stairs to begin a conversation that will inevitably lead to a relationship ending.

We all know this feeling well, and it's my judgment that what we do with it says much about who we are and how we live our lives. I used to avoid this feeling with intensity and purpose, my need for safety trumping all other experiences available to me in life's buffet. However over the years I have learned to balance on the ledge of fear and discomfort, to let them wash over me and through me, and to jump anyway (most of the time). Courage and fortitude are about feeling these emotions, leaning into them, and moving forward in spite of them. I had a philosophy professor in college who said to me once, "Success in life is directly correlated to your willingness to recognize what is necessary, and then do it — regardless of how uncomfortable it makes you." So simple, and yet so hard to do.

As I tried to still my numb and shaking hands so I could open my bear canister, I felt a momentary disappointment about not getting to experience this place in the daylight. Since I arrived at dark and would be leaving before sunup, my only exposure to this luxurious campsite would be vague shapes and bouncing patches of green and brown as I navigated with my headlamp.

And then it occurred to me — it should be getting light by now. I looked up at the sky — it was still ink black with millions of pinprick stars. I looked down at my watch and noted that it was 6:00 a.m. Weird. If not full dawn, the darkness should at least be slowly lifting.

For a few heartbeats I was stupefied, suspended in a space-time wrinkle that horrified and fascinated me. And then my critical thinking skills kicked in and the truth arrived in mundane and embarrassing fashion. My watch has two time settings, and for some reason I couldn't even remember "Time 2" was set two hours

Starry Night

The night sky is immeasurably beautiful once you get away from the lights of the city. The darkness comes alive with starlight, and the nuances of depth and distance can be felt if not fully seen or understood. Constellations are clearly visible, and The Milky Way is spread across the sky as if by some infinite butter knife. I have laid on my back for hours, staring into the void; there is something about touching the beginnings of everything that envelopes me in a wonderful yet overwhelming vertigo — as if for a brief second I can see the answer to every question that has ever been asked.

earlier. I also had the bad habit of bumping my watch into things and inadvertently switching to this mode. Grimacing, I pressed the button to illuminate my watch and quickly confirmed my suspicions. Sure enough, it was actually only 4:00 a.m.

I stood there, jerkily shaking in the sub-freezing darkness and took stock. I let myself momentarily fantasize about unpacking and going back to sleep for a couple hours, however this didn't make sense for a variety of reasons — not the least of which was that I already knew the quilt wouldn't keep me warm. I decided that my best option was to turn my headlamp to its brightest setting and start the day's journey.

The Sierras feel dangerous and wild when dappled by the sun, and by night this sense is heightened and intensified — particularly if you have an active imagination. As I found the trail and began my hike toward Muir Pass, I imagined I could hear the muffled hoof beats of Dark Riders in the distance, and that a swollen, voracious spider giant was stalking me. I actually welcomed these thoughts as they distracted me and made me feel like the warrior hero in an epic JMT adventure. This "lone-man-against-the-world" fantasy has always thrilled me, both because it speaks to my need to prove myself and because there is something about suffering that cleans the soul; as if each love lost or mountain climbed scrubs away a blemish. Does thinking this way mean I'm broken? Perhaps — but at least I can play with all the other discarded misfit toys who call themselves endurance athletes.

I was making my way slowly upward, switch-backing up the hillside below Evolution Lake. It wasn't light yet, but I was getting comfortable with my surroundings. I hadn't seen a living thing since waking up, and it was easy to feel like I was the only soul out there moving in the darkness. Then as I turned a corner, two high beam eyes flashed at me from the trail ahead. Instantly on high alert, my senses had also already absorbed the large, wooly shadow lurking behind the eyes — a bear — perhaps even more immense than the one that had pilfered my food!

"Stop looking at me, swan!"

Many animals, particularly those that explore at night, have a special reflective surface behind their eyes that help them see in the dark. It's called the tapetum lucidum, and it acts like a mirror, bouncing light back to the brain for a second look. Quite a few animals have this superpower, including dogs, cats, cattle, horses — and bears. Interestingly, all eyes glow different colors based on varying substances, retina pigments, and ages. Even two dogs of the same species can glare at you in the dark with different colors. Bear's night eyes generally look yellow, orange, or red (as if they aren't scary enough), however I have no recollection of what color they were on this night.

Before I could even formulate a coherent thought the bear raced off into the night, leaving me rooted to my spot in the trail, breathless and wide-eyed. Nice. I guess the JMT warrior hero was just too much man for him to handle. I shook myself, releasing the fight-or-flight energy that had come alive in my muscles and nerve endings and began moving once more.

As the morning lightened and the shadows around me finally began to materialize, I found myself in the middle of a desolate, rocky plain. The plains stretched on all sides until they eventually sprouted from the earth and became monolithic stone giants, stoically guarding one of Earth's last pristine bastions. In front of me the trail kept winding into the horizon, and I wondered if the pass I could see in the distance was real. This trail was booby-trapped with illusions and trickery, and countless times I reached the "top" of a mountain only to discover another, and another after that.

Muir Pass proved to be the wiliest of all the JMT passes, and the sun was fully unfurled by the time I had navigated its countless false passes. I stood below what could only be the final climb and watched curiously as a shadow danced on the hilltop above. There was a person up there, moving in an odd rhythm, arms and legs bouncing jauntily like a windup girl from Paolo Bacigalupi's futuristic masterpiece. As I made my way up, the figure continued the strange Sierra waltz.

I finally reached the top and was relieved to discover that it was the true pass after all. I also discovered the dancer was a tall, ageless Japanese man dressed in black.

We greeted each other, and he somehow communicated to me with short words and hand gestures that he was looking for someone wearing a Nike hat. I told him I hadn't seen anyone all morning, and that seemed to worry him. He then asked how long I was planning to be on the trail, and when I replied he nodded enthusiastically and said, "Seven days!" as he held up his pack that was just as small as mine — a fellow fast-packer.

If we could have communicated more effectively we may have had much to discuss, but it was mostly just awkward. And I have to say, particularly in hindsight, there was something unusual about him. Not sinister, but not normal. As if he were an angel or extraterrestrial that had taken human form to spend the morning on top of Muir Pass.

I was pleasantly surprised to see a stone hut on the pass, sitting small and sturdy on the saddle that straddled the world as far as the eye could see. I took off my pack for a brief rest and went to inspect the cabin. There was an etched plaque by the front door that read:

Muir Hut

This building was constructed in 1930 by the Sierra Club in cooperation with the Sierra National Forest and dedicated to the memory of John Muir.

The Muir Hut is intended as temporary shelter for hikers caught in storms on this exposed section of the trail.

I creaked open the door and looked inside. It was empty, clean, and simple; but I could imagine what a welcome sight it would be if the weather turned angry. Pretty cool. I had no idea this hut was here, or that it had been here weathering the elements for the last 83 years. It was also somewhat surreal to encounter a token of civilization, monastic as it was, out here in the middle of nowhere. I had that feeling multiple times during my trip, stimulated by anything from road signs to ranger stations. In the mountains I lost myself for hours on end, becoming nobody and everybody. I would often find myself speaking in strange accents or languages or laughing at the wind, and twice awoke with a certainty that I wasn't alone. Inexplicable, terrifying, magnificent things happen on the edge of the world if you are open to them. But then I would hear a voice or see a building and get yanked back to myself, left only with the lingering impression that I had just glimpsed something significant.

I took one last full circle look from 12,000 feet, waved to the Japanese man who was still stretching and looking back the way I'd come, and dropped onto the other side of the pass. It was steep and the trail was littered with rocks of all shapes and sizes, but I ran and let the momentum carry me down the mountain. As I sped my way down the slope I occasionally looked up from the treacherous path to admire the landscape below: The Range of Light. John Muir's favorite of the entire exquisite wilderness he explored. And I could see why. Barren and lonely, all sharp edges and dizzying openness, striking in its contrasts and enormity. More than anywhere else on the trail, the area south of Muir Pass gave me a sense of the forces of time and nature that created the Sierra Nevada range, and I smiled as I imagined John Muir thinking much the same thing as he careened down to the plain below.

Lost in the beauty and rhythm of rock skipping I was startled when I turned onto a switchback and saw the Japanese man right behind me. He had given no sign at the top of being prepared to leave, and I was running — how was he suddenly on my heels? As we continued to descend the trail repeatedly wound back on itself, and I was able to catch glimpses of him. He remained 5-10 feet behind me, focused and quiet, using trekking poles to fall down the mountain in a spidery shamble that looked even stranger than his hilltop dance; but his technique was effective, and he stayed with me easily.

This ignited my competitive juices, and I started to run faster. I hadn't experienced that feeling while on the trail, and I welcomed its power. I hurtled recklessly from mound to stone, enjoying the contest and companionship. Then all of a sudden I turned a corner and the man was gone. Vanished. There was nowhere he could have turned off, so he had either fallen soundlessly from the cliff or stopped for some reason. I peered back up the trail, looked down at the rocks below, but didn't see anything human — very odd. I shrugged and kept moving.

Ten minutes later I slowed to cross a stream and was again surprised to see the man behind me once more. What the hell? Where had he gone and how had he caught me, particularly with the speed I was going? We nodded at each other, and I shook my head in disbelief, more confused than annoyed. We crossed the stream together and fell into a blistering pace once more.

And then he disappeared again — this time for good. After which I dubbed him "The Mountain Ninja". I know what you're thinking, but I am virtually certain he was a real person, and I have no idea how he defied the laws of physics or from what universe he came. Perhaps some mysteries aren't meant to be solved.

The Mountain Ninja had reminded me how good it felt to run, and through this process I discovered that my legs and lungs had finally strengthened enough to let it rip. I realized that for the entire trip I had been thinking of myself as a backpacker trying to run instead of a runner carrying a pack. This may seem like an insignificant distinction, but reminding myself that I am a runner had an immediate impact. I loosened my body, increased my cadence, and thought about the myriad trail miles I had covered leading up to this point. For this first time on the JMT, I simply ran.

I ran for what seemed like five or six miles, although in looking back I doubt it was that far. Then at some point I misjudged a step and felt a jolt of pain in my left leg. At the time the pain barely registered, as the part of me that would care was quite literally shut off. I was aware of this phenomenon sporadically while on the trail, but I didn't really think about it till later. I imagine it was similar to what a fighter must experience — extreme focus on the task at hand and the complete exclusion of everything unproductive like hurt or doubt. Some small part of my consciousness was aware of thirst, pain, hunger, and fatigue, but I truly didn't feel them or even acknowledge them — at least until this point in the trip.

The trail eventually leveled out, and I decided to save some energy reserves and drop back into a fast hike. That's when I noticed how tired I felt. For the only time I could remember on this trail, I was… weary. I also noticed how incredibly hot it was. I had begun the day by braving temperatures in the 20's, and now it felt at least 90. A 65-degree temperature swing and a 12,000-foot pass over 10 hours and almost 20 miles. No wonder I was tired. And that twinge in my leg just wouldn't go away. Every time I stepped down a sharp sting shot all the way up my leg. I don't know why, and it was probably a combination of things, but this time I failed to see the rabbit hole coming and tumbled head-first into its unknown depths.

I spent the next few hours grumpily winding my way toward Mather Pass. Once again, I reminded myself of my dog; when we let him out in the rain he raises his eyebrows incredulously, eyes the evil downpour, and then slowly and dramatically tiptoes outside. I wasn't tiptoeing, but my pace had slowed considerably. I began thinking about my mileage totals and my mood darkened further. I would do the calculations when I stopped for the evening, but I knew I was way off pace and that this would present some very real concerns.

The trail became even steeper as I entered the last push before the pass. I had internalized the landscape over these days on the trail and my body was used to its rhythm. I found that I knew what was coming without looking at the map: a flat valley, a rolling uphill, a steep climb to a pass, a treacherous slope straight down, repeat. I generally don't mind going uphill as it challenges me and offers a welcome change of pace, however this section took every ounce of tenacity I could muster. My leg was becoming excruciating, and it was all I could do to focus on anything else.

My negativity was fully illuminated when I bumped into three Cal Poly students who were on their third day of a 90-mile loop. They were energetic and fun, and one of them was wearing a Cinderella 50K race shirt. I had done that race earlier in the year, and we briefly chatted about it. It turns out they were also triathletes and annually competed at Wildflower, a triathlon festival close to Cal Poly. I started the Sacramento Team in Training program that trains for Wildflower, and I met my wife during this process. Our first kiss was at a training weekend for Wildflower, and I proposed there on the same spot. I even qualified for Nationals for the first time at Wildflower. Running into these kids should have been serendipitous and wonderful. It should have connected me to home and filled me with gratitude and the certainty that we are all woven together in the tapestry of life. But I didn't feel any of these things. I envied their youthful exuberance and camaraderie. I spoke about my leg and slow pace when they asked me how my trip was going. I ended the interaction as quickly as I could.

I eventually shuffled my way to Palisade Lakes, and while I failed to acknowledge it at the time, they were beautiful. I was really hoping to make it up and over Mather Pass before dark, but with my hurt leg and another five miles to go it didn't seem possible. I also didn't know if I could find water or flat ground if I had to camp on the pass. The undercurrent flowing beneath these "good" reasons was a deep desire to stop moving, so I decided to call it a day.

I passed the first lake and started looking for a place to camp when I hit the second lake minutes later. The trail wound along a hillside above the lake, so I was concerned about finding flat ground and water access here as well. I eventually located a small plateau that overlooked the lake, and if I was willing to scramble cross-country for a few hundred yards I could reach the water. Good enough.

It was only five o'clock so I was able to make camp in full daylight. Rather than enjoy the extra time and sun setting over the lake, I sat on a rock and sulked. I got out my maps and figured out where I was and how far I had yet to go: 77 miles to Whitney Portal. I had been hoping to finish tomorrow or at the very worst the next day. Both were impossible. Particularly with my leg slowing me down. It actually occurred to me that my leg may be broken, and I really didn't know what to do about that. I would run out of food, I may not be able to connect with my dad for pickup, and I would miss important work on Monday. Even if I decided to quit I would still have to get to civilization somehow. I looked at my maps for potential routes out. There wasn't anything close by; in fact the two best options would require cresting passes and hiking at least 30 miles. Sad, frustrated, and confused, I was convinced that my trip was over.

As dark as this time was for me, I am immensely proud of the mental strength I found that night. Some steely part of me that had been forged since the last time I pit myself against this trail was unmoved by the hopelessness. It stood apart and watched the drama with understanding and amusement. Even while mired in this negative feedback loop, I was able to stay mindful and recognize the meltdown for what it was. All was not lost. Solutions could be found. I couldn't see or touch them at the moment, but I had faith that perspective and answers would come. I crawled into my tarp-tent while the sun's last rays were still twinkling on the lake below and committed to shifting my energy in the morning. I would give myself this pity-party tonight, but tomorrow I would find my way home.

Pity Parties: productive or potentially problematic?

The idea of opening myself to the hopelessness of a situation is uncomfortable and foreign to me, particularly in light of my feelings about the power of positive thinking. However it seems as if embracing a difficult encounter, holding it even as it holds you, somehow lessens its influence; and I think mindfullness is the key to feeling the despair without letting it take hold completely. If I can maintain an awareness that there may be a disconnect between reality and my current perception of it, then I can move on quickly once the wave of negative emotion has crashed and subsided.

Chapter 11
The Mayor

(Day 6 — Palisade Lakes to Rae Lakes, 26 miles)

"When we are no longer able to change a situation, we are challenged to change ourselves."
— Viktor Frankl

Strange dreams were a regular occurrence on this JMT adventure — no doubt my subconscious diligently working to compile and assign meaning to the barrage of experiences and introspections. On this night I dreamt I was a prisoner in some *Orange is the New Black* co-ed alternate universe. What did this mean? Was I captive to my injured leg or perhaps my limiting beliefs? Was it simply my fear of failure or the unknown manifesting itself tangibly? The latter is highly possible as I have always harbored a deep terror at the thought of going to prison. Besides the obvious reasons to avoid incarceration, there is also something about living a life without purpose and passion that makes my skin crawl. We are all meant to be free in every sense of the word — I feel this so strongly that it sometimes bubbles up and makes me want to scream like a boiling tea kettle.

Regardless of what my sleeping brain was trying to convey to me, I awoke with a refreshed sense of peace and determination. I still had no idea how I was going to complete this quest, or what I would do if my leg got worse; but the only choice available to me was to suck it up and figure it out. It is simple and powerful to have no escape routes and walk the tightrope of life and death — not that I ever really felt like my life was on the line, but my decisions while alone in the wild directly affected my safety and ability to find my way home.

I somewhat leisurely ate breakfast and purified water that I had collected the day before. Then, before putting my gear away I took my maps over to the same rock I had sulked on the previous evening. I sat, took a deep breath, and consciously stepped into what I could do rather than focusing on what I couldn't. I broke the problem into smaller pieces (what my business coach would call "small chunking") and wrote them down on the back of my mileage chart.

FINISHING BY SUNDAY

With 77 miles to go, I could cover roughly 25 miles a day for the next three days. That would get me to Whitney Portal sometime Sunday afternoon. After which I still had a solid six-hour trip back home, including picking up my car in Tuolumne Meadows. I wouldn't have much time to sleep or reconnect with Jen, but it was do-able. I was leading a group and meeting with a new client on Monday and was absolutely dedicated to honoring these commitments. In hindsight, my unwillingness to consider missing work may have been influenced by the self-sabotaging trickster in my brain, which tried to give me an excuse to quit in the name of good business.

GETTING PICKED UP AT THE END

On Saturday afternoon I would send another pre-programmed message letting my dad know that I was 24 hours from the finish. That's how we were planning to communicate anyway — it would just be two days later than expected. As long as I continued to send my daily "check-ins" my family's fears would hopefully be assuaged.

Simple Pleasures

In looking back I realize the simplicity of survival is one of my primary motivators for spending long hours in the backcountry. The multitudes of daily decisions in my normal life distract me, but figuring out what font to use or which ringtone I like somehow cheapens the experience of living. I yearn to pit my body against the elements, build shelter, and hunt and be hunted. It's not adrenaline I seek — surfing 100-foot waves or climbing El Capitan sound insane to me — but instead connection to my roots; to what's really important; to what feels like true nourishment for my soul. Does this stem from something unique inside me, or is it bigger than that? Is it in all of us? Is it something deeply embedded in our genetic codes? I certainly can't speak for you, but I would argue that the more we simplify, the richer our lives become.

FOOD

Food — a very real concern. Even if I rationed food I would run out completely by tomorrow afternoon. This meant summiting Whitney after a severely limited caloric intake followed by a complete 24-hour fast. At home this would simply be uncomfortable. Out here, exposed to extreme elevation and temperatures, moving quickly from dawn to dusk with all my possessions on my back — it probably wouldn't be life threatening but it definitely wasn't ideal. I was conservatively burning 6,000-8,000 calories per day while on the JMT and had already been operating at a deficit all week. I decided to eat only when absolutely necessary and to ask other hikers for food.

LEG

I would have to play this by ear; but since I couldn't easily hike out from here anyway, my only choice was to keep moving. I know pain and was fairly confident that I could grind my way out, particularly if the alternatives were dying alone in the mountains or an expensive and embarrassing search and rescue mission. My sister hiked around Europe for weeks without realizing her ankle was broken. My wife broke her arm and then competed at a triathlon National Championship the next weekend. I thought about them and about how they might both be thinking about me at the same moment, and that made my internal fire burn a little brighter. I resolved to do whatever was necessary not to let them down.

Once I had worked through the logistics and touched hope, I felt as if a great weight had been lifted off my shoulders. Whether I was willing to acknowledge it or not, some part of me had always been aware that my pace was too slow — and this reality became heavier each day. Now I felt light and clear, infused with the power of an attainable goal.

Goal, goal, goal, goal!

As previously mentioned, having clear goals that motivate and excite you is one the most basic and effective tools for achieving success. Goals by their very nature are most efficacious when they push you out of your comfort zone, however there is a fine line between a "stretch" goal and an unrealistic goal. A stretch goal lies in the far reaches of your universe, but there is enough internal and external evidence to support it so you believe it's possible. Completing the JMT in six days was a perfect stretch goal before my shoes hit dirt. But when I actually began my battle with the mountains that six-day goal gradually began to feel out of reach — and an unrealistic goal has little luster or potency and is nothing but a wish in the wind.

Content with my new plan, I quickly finished my morning tasks and began my climb toward Mather Pass. I immediately found a flowing rhythm, and in short order I left the lakes below and the trees became hunched and sparse. I smiled at the beauty of all things and my place amongst them, and then cocked my head slightly as I suddenly had two significant realizations.

1. Mindset is everything. Twelve hours ago I was ready to commit seppuku and would have complained about the tax burden if I'd been given a winning lottery ticket. Now, under virtually identical circumstances, I was thoroughly enjoying myself.

2. There was no pain in my leg. Zero.

Incredible. I briefly wondered whether my bad attitude had caused my leg pain, and if my current positivity had cured it. Or perhaps being pain-free had simply allowed room for the new perspective. I decided it didn't matter — the important and amazing piece of information was that my leg definitely wasn't broken, and may not even be seriously injured. After returning home I thought more about this odd happenstance, and I can honestly say I have no idea why my leg hurt so badly or how it healed itself so quickly. Maybe the JMT is a vortex for strange solar energy like the Bermuda Triangle. Maybe I have a guardian angel with a knack for orthopedics. Like so many things on this trip and in life, I will never know.

Caught in the steady current of blissful reverie, I crested Mather Pass without the usual climax and fanfare. I didn't realize it at the time, but at 12,080 feet above sea level I was now standing higher than I had at any point on this trip so far. With barely a pause, I began my descent. It wouldn't be the usual freefall — I knew from studying the map that I would be rolling up and down for the next 10 miles until reaching Pinchot Pass. Without the pressure of trying to travel almost 40 miles a day, I felt free to relax and simply enjoy myself.

My creativity came to life, and I found myself writing a new book in my head. What began as a fun exercise quickly developed into a path I didn't want to lose, and I stopped frequently to scribble breadcrumb notes to myself. In fact twice I actually fished out my phone from the top compartment of my pack, turned it on, and left voice recordings of chapter outlines. This is a fairly regular occurrence for me, even on trail runs at home. I am an idea machine. Something about the way I'm built coupled with being in business for myself keeps that lever pushed full throttle. And when I'm running that part of me spreads its wings and takes flight, stimulated by endorphins and freedom.

But that creativity can have a dark side as well. Eventually my ideas for the book were spent, and my mind roamed other landscapes. I began to wonder if I could make it to Whitney by Sunday, even with the new strategy. I imagined taking a side trail up ahead, hiking out, and seeing Jen's face tomorrow; or hearing her laugh — not the indulgent chuckle she sometimes gives me when I'm trying to be funny but the spontaneous and wonderful full-bodied laugh that bursts from her when she's truly amused. This is another kind of rabbit hole, but one just as dangerous. And while I didn't fall completely into this one, I unknowingly clung to the ledge by only my fingertips, feet dangling above the abyss below.

As I physically wound my way toward Pinchot Pass, mentally I began hedging my bets and backpedaling from success. I told myself that the destination wasn't the important part and that the true purpose of this trip (and life) was being willing to make the attempt and experiencing the journey. I thought about all the condolences I would receive for almost reaching my goal and how martyred and morally superior I would feel to work so hard for something that wouldn't be realized. I am ashamed to admit that this was a comfortable space for me, and for a time I swam in these warm waters and explored their depths.

And then my mindfulness saved me once more. That same part of me that had reminded me to have hope the night before yanked me roughly out of the water and slapped me backhand across the face.

"What are you doing?" it demanded, voice low and fierce.

All of a sudden my whole perspective shifted, as if I had just been manhandled and lifted upside down by a mountain troll. What seemed like keen, self-actualized perception and insight that can only be tapped by the fully evolved was now tainted by the truth. My brain had been trying to sabotage me again. And I realized with horror that I knew those waters so well because I had swum their currents countless times before. For whatever reason I identified myself as the guy who "almost gets things done" or "makes the best of a bad situation." And while I could rationally say I didn't want to be this man, some deeper, less secure part of me clearly kept purposefully wiggling this loose tooth and reveling in the familiar pain. Inexplicably, I was afraid of success.

As all of these realizations crashed down on me, I was reminded of one of my favorite quotes (which I and many others associate with Nelson Mandela but actually belongs to Marianne Williamson): "Our deepest fear is that we are powerful beyond measure. It is our light, not our darkness, that most frightens us."

Those words have always resonated with the softly-strumming chords of my soul. It is so much easier for me to be not quite good enough and to remain wrapped in the snug cloak of angst. My life was littered with the wreckage of self-imposed roadblocks. But I didn't want to be that man anymore, and I could see my light shining up ahead, just waiting for me to step into it. I realized that I had just arrived at the moment this trip was designed to create. Would I choose the well-worn path or the unknown road that wound treacherously upward and scared me with its heights? I looked at both, and I felt the common road beckoning to me with secure intimacy. My spiritual foot hovered above the trail for what seemed like eternity, and then I made my choice.

"Fuck that. I'm finishing this thing," I said out loud.

And with that declaration I actually felt my spirit lift and expand like the Kraken bursting from the ocean in *Clash of the Titans* (a tad trite perhaps, but accurate nonetheless).

Stepping into my power suffused the day with added brightness and extra hue, and I marveled at the beauty surrounding me: Lake Marjorie's deep turquoise waters; Pinchot Pass and its towering panoramas; a sweet downhill section. I passed a large group of backpackers who were carrying overloaded packs, slowly making their way up the mountain I had just descended. I recognized the hopeless looks in their eyes and painful hitches in their gaits and was filled with gratitude for my lightweight pack. What a blessing it was to not feel my spine compressing or strain with every uphill step.

Eventually I arrived at the valley floor and was surprised to find a wood and metal suspension bridge spanning a large river. I had been in Sequoia & Kings Canyon National Park for two days, and it continued to impress me. Not only was the landscape spectacular, but the trails were maintained and marked better than anywhere else on the JMT.

I crossed the bridge and turned up the valley toward Rae Lakes some six-miles ahead. Most valleys in the Sierras are green and forested, fed by the snowmelt that runs down them. However this dale was perhaps the most spectacular of them all. I didn't even notice the gradual uphill, and I steadily ticked off the miles.

About an hour before sunset, I reached the first of Rae Lakes. Breathtaking. A bowl cut right into the rock, serrated cliffs shooting straight up from the water for hundreds of feet, and emerald waters reflecting the lushness surrounding it. I had already resolved to bring my family up here, and that became a promise.

In short order I reached the second and larger of the lakes and began to casually look for a place to set up for the night. I passed a couple potential campsites, but they didn't speak to me and I wanted to make it further before stopping. The trail would parallel the lake for almost two miles and then turn right and shoot up toward Glen Pass, and I wanted to get as close to the pass as I could tonight.

The lake seemed to stretch on forever, and I kept moving. I hadn't seen any place to camp for some time and just as I was about to question the wisdom of my strategy I heard voices off the trail to my right. Then it occurred to me that I was hungry and had yet to ask anyone for food. I didn't particularly feel like begging, but this was clearly an opportunity.

I walked toward the voices, and after weaving through a maze of large boulders found two men setting up a tent.

"Hey, guys. How's it going?" I offered with a smile.

"Good, man," said one of the men, nodding. They seemed friendly, but remained focused on their task.

I looked around and noted the enormity of the campsite. It was practically big enough for a Boy Scouts Jamboree.

"Do you mind if I set up over there? I haven't really talked to anyone other than myself for a few days, and I'm not that interesting," I said and pointed to a spot 30-feet away.

They both laughed and looked up from the tent poles they were putting together, and the other man said, "Sure, dude. The more the merrier. We don't really like each other anyway so it might be good to have you around."

I returned their laugh, thanked them, and went to set up my home for the evening.

As I was unloading my pack, two more men walked up carrying water. I quickly noted four packs leaning up against a log and realized this party was bigger than I thought.

It can be uncomfortable and awkward to try to pierce the bubble of friendship and closeness when you are standing outside of it, and as such I found myself lingering in the area I had staked out. As I was trying to decide how and if I was going to ask for food, one of the new guys called over to me.

"We're about to sit down to eat if you're interested in joining us."

And so began a completely unexpected and enjoyable night. Three public defenders and a business owner, they were long-time friends that met for a backpacking trip every summer. Funny, sarcastic, intelligent, and introspective, they reminded me of my friends and welcomed me as one of their own. Even better, upon hearing my tale they showered me with eats that I didn't have to ask for. Typical backpackers, they had all brought way too much food, and I actually had to turn most of it down.

They were planning to sleep in the following morning, so I said my good-byes before retiring to my tent. One of the men appeared to be the leader of the group — one of those things we all recognize from our pack ancestry but have trouble putting into words — and I particularly connected with him. We exchanged contact information, and he laughed as I read his email address and raised my eyebrows.

"Yeah — I'm the mayor," he said with a casual shrug.

"Cool," I replied, matching his blasé.

When it comes down to it, we are all just people who want to learn, grow, and love; to touch something magical that we yearn for but don't understand; to be the best versions of ourselves we can be, even if that sometimes scares us. And the mountains magnify this exquisitely.

Coffers full and spirits lifted, I went to bed content and excited to start the final stretch of my journey.

Chapter 12
Gang Fight

(Day 7 — Rae Lakes to Crabtree Ranger Station, 31 miles)

"Sometimes you just have to dance to the music that's playing."
— Seely Booth, Bones

As the first rays of morning sun reached me I was halfway up Glen Pass, having already skirted the remainder of the lake and risen almost a thousand feet toward the stars. As I wound upward, I often looked back at the spectacular view below and became freshly dazzled each time, as if I was a junkie and these mountains my fix. It occurred to me that I would have missed this splendor if I'd been persuaded by my demons and hiked out, and I felt a pang of melancholy as I momentarily touched all the other opportunities that had gone unclaimed throughout my life. This feeling wasn't regret exactly, but rather an acknowledgement and acceptance of the winding path that had brought me to this moment: 34-years-old, standing hungry, cold, and exhilarated below Glen Pass on a Saturday morning in September.

Around 8:00 a.m. I reached the top. Glen Pass is unique in that it juts from the earth like the spine of some gargantuan, mutant brontosaurus. I straddled the world for a time as I hopped the vertebrae rocks.

I squinted into the morning sun, felt the crisp air on my face and in my lungs, and was purely and singularly alive.

Glen Pass was the second-to-last pass I would have to face, and only 36 miles from the top of Mount Whitney. For the first time since I had hatched this crazy JMT idea years before, I could actually see the finish line. What had begun as an amorphous and intangible hope had solidified and matured and was now just one day from fruition. A dizzying sense of perspective enveloped me, followed by a jumbled rush of excited emotion. With success almost in my grasp, my feet started moving just a little faster.

I spent the next five miles in a downhill euphoria, and when the trees started to expand and multiply into a sea of green, I knew I had almost reached Bubbs Creek. I would soon turn left and begin meandering up a valley that would eventually lead to Forester Pass, which is the last and highest pass on the JMT; a pass that I had history with and grudging respect for.

On my first John Muir Trail attempt a decade ago, I began my trip below Mount Whitney and hiked north. I wasn't a trained endurance athlete and was carrying a ludicrous amount of weight. I trudged painfully and slowly for a couple days, constantly trying to fight off rain, mosquitoes, and crippling negativity. On the third day I finally reached the base of Forester Pass (my first and only pass on that trip), and decided to stop for the evening.

The terrain was barren and merciless, and I precariously stretched my tarp between rocks. Just as I had placed the last stone, the skies opened with fury and soaked me to my core. I distinctly remember laying there awake all night, shivering in my wet sleeping bag. The rain pelted straight down with such force that my tarp was plastered to my body and I could feel each droplet, as if Zeus had sent an army of tiny minions to attack me with machine-water guns. Every now and then the world exploded with crashing thunder, shaking the rock beneath me, and lightning illuminated and electrified the night. It was awful, but so uniquely visceral that I also had to appreciate it on some level — after all, how many people could say they had spent a night in a lightning storm at the top of the world?

The next morning the sky was clear, but my mood remained dark. I hefted my pack (which was even heavier because of the water that had saturated everything) onto my shoulders, and slogged my way up Forester's innumerable switchbacks. Each step brought me closer to my breaking point, and by the time I reached the top I had convinced myself to abandon the adventure. You know the rest. So while I had technically climbed Forester before, it would be a stretch to say I'd conquered it. On this new expedition I was curious and excited to see the pass through more seasoned eyes.

Many passes on the JMT somewhat harmlessly wind upward for miles, and then get rocky and steep near the top. Forester is not one of those passes. Soon after turning up the valley I felt the environment harden. Gone were the warm greens and yellows that made it easy to feel like I was in the Shire and might see Bilbo or Frodo sauntering toward me with a friendly smile and a plate of treats. Instead it started to feel like a grim march to Mordor as I entered a gray world of sharp edges and shadows.

The terrain quickly became steep, and the oxygen scarce. I was breathing hard, feeling the burn of exertion in the bellies of my leg muscles and deep in my lungs. I topped rise after rise, and I was reminded of Muir Pass and its host of false passes. Except this was higher, longer, and more difficult. I embraced the struggle however as this was my final pass, and I wanted to fully experience everything Forester could throw at me and see what I was made of. Similar to a batter wanting to hit against the best pitcher in the league when he has his best stuff, I wanted to earn my way to that sign on the pinnacle of the pass that read "13,200 feet".

I eventually began climbing a great, stone staircase and felt a tingle of excitement because I remembered it from my last trip. It was near the top. Inhaling and exhaling rapidly, sweat dripping from the band of my hat, I was surprised when I caught two other backpackers who had stopped for a rest.

"We're earning this aren't we?" I huffed.

"Nothing better," drawled one of the men, and then toasted me with a bottle of whiskey and took a deep drink.

He must have seen the horror on my face, because he smiled wanly and said, "Don't know how else I'd get up this thing."

I raised my eyebrows and nodded the way you would at someone dancing naked in the street who had just asked for a million dollars, and I kept pushing skyward.

I climbed and climbed, and eventually stopped trying to make out the top and instead stared at the rock beneath my feet. If I just kept taking one more step, I would get there sooner or later. And then the ground leveled out and a gust of icy wind blasted me from the south. I had finally achieved the pass.

If Forester and I were heavyweight foes locked in a cosmic boxing rematch, I was proud of how this fight unfolded. The first contest had battered me so severely that I lost my will to win, but this time I had delivered just as much punishment as I'd received. A draw was the most I could hope for in a battle with this mountain — you don't defeat something as ancient and forbidding as Forester. Nor would I want to. As much as I like finding obstacles and overcoming them, I am also warmed by the comfort of all things having a place they belong. The world just feels right when the Yankees are in first place; when my dad can beat me at one-on-one basketball; and when Forester Pass is indomitable. This may hearken back to the pack dynamics I noticed in the mayor's group. I am generally in charge of my domain and lay claim to the countryside of my life — perhaps it gives me succor to encounter a wolf even larger than I am, and to let go of the need to have it all figured out. Maybe it's even more than that. Maybe it's divine. All I know is that reverence fills and frees me.

As colossal as this mountain was, the pass was little more than a few wingspans of rocky ground. I was a bit taken aback to discover that three other people were sharing this outcrop with me, and that one of them was talking on a cell phone! Instead of annoying me like before, feeling civilization's touch at the top of this desolate protrusion infused me with hope. After all the physical and emotional miles traveled, I felt like I'd been out here for years, and the thought of hearing my wife's voice made my heart pound even faster.

I set my pack against a boulder, pulled out my phone, and turned it on. Then I held it in front of my face and squinted at it like an old man, waiting impatiently to see if I had service. My phone loaded slowly, minutes passed, and eventually my heart sank as my fear became a reality. "No service" stood small but proudly mocking me in the top right corner of the display. I must have been a pitiful sight, slumping there dejectedly staring at my phone as I willed service bars to appear.

"As long as you're quick, you can use mine," said the voice of an angel.

I looked up slowly as if coming out of a dream, and the man who had been talking on his phone was now holding it out toward me.

"Seriously? You are the man! I would love to talk to my wife for a minute if that's cool," I stammered.

"Sure thing, man. I get it. That's what I just did, but she has to pick me up a day early so we need to get moving like yesterday," he said with a grin.

"Got it. Two minutes," I replied as I took the phone and began dialing her number.

The phone rang. Two rings. Three. She wasn't going to answer. This was a number she didn't recognize, and I would get sent to the dark dungeon of voicemail.

"Hello?"

Her voice! And an explosion of emotion that I can't even begin to describe hit me. In hindsight this experience reminded me of *Survivor* and how the contestants always cry when their family members send them videos or show up unexpectedly. Jen and I have often wondered why they are so moved to strong emotion, but I think I understand it now. When you are fighting for days or weeks against an unforgiving and unknown adversary, you put the fragile, vulnerable part of yourself that just wants to be seen and loved into a locked chest in your heart. Over time walls and moats are built around this lockbox and the whole area becomes overgrown with foliage; but then out of nowhere a brother's written encouragement, a best friend's touch, a wife's voice, and the chest and all of its defenses blow away like sand in the wind.

"Hi baby! I'm standing on top of Forester Pass and borrowing somebody else's phone. It's so good to hear your voice," I shouted over the whistling wind.

In all honesty, I don't remember exactly what we talked about because the moment was infused with such powerful sentiment. I know I did most of the talking, trying to connect with her and share my whole trip in a jubilant rush of words and thoughts. (No doubt she will chuckle as she reads this because I often do this in our "normal" lives.) I conveyed how much I loved and missed her, and asked her to tell my dad to pick me up the next day around 1:00 p.m. And then before either of us knew what had happened, I was handing the phone back to its owner.

For a second I just stood there, breathing deeply, letting the ache of being both here and there run through me. And then I refocused on the present moment and the task at hand.

I profusely thanked my phone benefactor, and we chatted briefly as he and his friend prepared to continue toward Whitney. They had been on the trail a couple weeks, and they would now have to move faster right at the end to make their pickup. I noted their large packs and bodies, and I wondered how difficult the trip had been for them up to this point. They would be trying to move as fast as me, which seemed unlikely, but I wished them luck as they began their descent.

Now I was alone except for a young woman who had been sitting silently on a rock above the trail.

"Can I offer you a grapefruit?" she asked with a look of playful naivety that only seems to exist in the very young or idealistically wild.

I studied her for a second and realized with chagrin that she was a ranger. This girl was probably in diapers while I was learning to drive, and here she was relaxing on this towering spike with a badge and gun. "I'm getting old," I thought.

"A grapefruit sounds amazing, but I don't really want to carry the weight," I replied, breaking one of my trail rules by turning down offered food. I didn't feel like trying to peel and eat the citrus fruit at the moment, and I really didn't want to add anything else to my pack.

"Hmm. I think I have some chocolate-covered almonds left. How about some of those?" she offered and turned to look in her pack.

"Now we're talking," I said through a smirk.

She managed to locate the treats, and I remained on the pass long enough to devour them. Just as I was wishing her well and turning to continue on my way, the whiskey drinkers from down below crested the pass. They knew the ranger. In fact, they were retired rangers and had been exploring these mountains longer than I'd been alive. If I felt old talking to the young ranger, these grizzled trail veterans must have felt prehistoric talking to us. I was reminded that in all things our perceptions, attitudes, and feelings are almost entirely shaped by our perspectives.

Ready to be on my way, I bid farewell to the three friends and then turned toward the narrow trail. I navigated through a short maze of rock and then found myself teetering thousands of feet above a vast stone desert, dotted with an occasional swath of blue or green.

Having vanquished my last pass, spoken to Jen, and enjoyed a few chocolate morsels, I was figuratively (and literally I suppose) on top of the world. I pointed myself downward and began moving with haste — and faster than I had at any point on the trail. Like a horse that knows it's almost at the barn, I felt the call of Whitney and responded.

Downward I flew, reveling in the sweet fluidity of the movement and noting how much more strong and agile I had become during these sustained backcountry days. I had prepared like a champion, but

Landscape of the mind

All those years ago I had camped and braved the elements on the plain below, however it looked foreign now. The picture in my mind didn't match the landscape before me, and I wondered whether the terrain was different or whether my memory had taken a little poetic license. The answer is obvious, and it's scary and humbling to think about how easy and common it is for our brains to deceive us. Memory research shows that when we remember something we actually rebuild it each time; so the more we access the memory the more degraded it becomes, until eventually it is entirely of our own creation. I challenge you (and myself) to remember this the next time you're "sure" of something!

even long trail hours at home couldn't fully simulate this experience, and my body was adapting to the new stimulus. Already lean, my abs were now chiseled into my shirt like Batman and my leg muscles pushed the veins tight against my skin.

In what felt like minutes I reached the base of the mountain and began moving swiftly across the exposed plain. I had developed a routine over the week where I would run while descending and then slow to a fast hike once the terrain leveled off — but this time I kept running. The path was cut narrowly into the patchy grass and stone, and often times I felt like I was gliding along a massive tightrope, occasionally wobbling from the chaos of momentum.

I quickly caught my friends who had just been on Forester, and I had to leave the trail to get around them. They were sitting in the middle of the path filling their bottles with archaic water pumps. They barely glanced at me and didn't say a word, but the looks on their faces told a clear story. If they truly had to reach Whitney Portal by tomorrow they were in trouble. I had empathy for their situation and wanted to help, but ultimately they could rely on nothing but their own legs and tenacity. I offered a few kind words and sped on.

I passed the turnoff to Shepherd Pass, entered a wooded forest, and then rolled up and down for five miles. It was incredible to think about the throng of microclimates and ecosystems I passed through each day, and it gave me a real sense of just how far I was traveling. It was not uncommon for the wet warmth of a valley meadow to be separated from an exposed, lifeless ridge by only a handful of heartbeats.

Suddenly a sign appeared just off the trail to my left. Other than the sign at the very beginning of the trail which listed a variety of possible destinations, no other sign had mentioned anything but the next landmark. But this sign read "Mt. Whitney, 13 miles" in clear print, white paint against dark brown wood. Thirteen miles. Wow. All the preparation, training, mental gymnastics, and emotional turmoil — and now I was a half-marathon away from standing on Whitney. Glen Pass had given me a pinhole view of success, Forester had widened it, and this little sign tore the hole so large that I could step through it and touch the end of the journey.

Smiling broadly, I looped my thumbs under my shoulder straps and began trotting southward once more. The changes to my body, the appreciation for how far I was going and what an accomplishment that was, and the unshakable conviction that success was inevitable — it was a little more than my capricious ego could handle. I began to feel invincible. As I've noted before, when I start to puff up and stick out my chest something always seems to quickly balance the scales. Of course this time was no different.

I was secure with my heading and hadn't checked my maps all day, but I assumed that I'd be traveling downhill till I reached Crabtree Ranger Station. So I was surprised and worried when I began climbing steep switchbacks. I pulled out my maps, and sure enough — there were a few precipitous ridges to ascend before finishing for the day. Slightly annoyed at the increased effort and time, I shrugged and continued the upward march.

That was when I felt a tickle on my nose. And then another on my eyelash. Confused, I looked around and quickly realized that it was snowing! Minutes before the sky had been clear and now dark clouds roiled with foreboding. I'd heard horror stories about the perilous and unpredictable weather patterns in the Sierras, but I'd never truly experienced them for myself and assumed they were mostly hyperbole. Snow wasn't necessarily the end of the world, but I was instantly concerned for a few reasons.

- Snowfall can cover tracks and change topography enough to make trails disappear — even wide and well-worn paths like the JMT.

- Mt. Whitney is the highest point in the continental United States. Climbing to the top in a whiteout would be impossible. If this storm didn't clear by tomorrow I would be stuck out here.

- I had to spend another night in this unforgiving wilderness and my quilt had already proven faulty. Tonight would be dangerously cold.

The temperature had dropped enough to make me shudder slightly and my fingers numb, despite the rapid uphill pace. I stopped to don my rain jacket and gloves, and shot a snarky and incredulous video journal entry acknowledging nature's ability to put me in my place. And then I did the only thing I could do — I kept moving.

As I made my way toward Crabtree — straight up, straight down, straight up again — the powder continued to fall. It never intensified into a blizzard, but the trail was slowly getting swallowed up and the temperature kept plummeting.

Eventually I spotted the turnoff to the ranger station, but not before I'd had plenty of time to consider my predicament and become thoroughly worried. I didn't think it would get cold enough to be deadly tonight … at least I hoped it wouldn't. But even if dawn didn't find me ice-crusted and lifeless (I may have morbidly pictured this on more than one occasion) the best-case scenario was that I would be extremely uncomfortable. I decided to ask the ranger if I could find a corner inside the station to hole up for the night. I'd never heard of anyone doing this, but it might save my life to ask.

I crossed a partially frozen stream, and then passed a handful of scattered tents that were arranged haphazardly. You can always tell whether people camping in the same vicinity know each other by how their tents are organized — even if tents are very close together (which only happens if space is limited), they generally belong to separate parties unless the entrances are facing each other and surrounding a cooking stone or campfire. And this happens everywhere in similar but different ways. It's fascinating how people make and break connection, establish boundaries, and create meaning. It seems as if the room we leave between ourselves and others, both emotionally and physically, is in direct proportion to the intimacy that exists; as if sharing time and an open heart literally draws us closer to each other.

The trail was now completely covered by fresh snow, however I could see the ranger station 200 yards south. I walked fast to keep my body temperature as high as possible and covered the gap quickly. Even from a distance, it felt deserted, and as I got closer I could see that the windows were covered by large sheets of plywood. It must be closed for the season, but was that movement on the front porch?

Someone was swaying in a rocking chair by the front door of the ranger station, and as I walked up I saw that it was a mature woman decked out in full REI paraphernalia. She had a whimsical smile on her face and seemed to be expecting me. Perhaps I had prematurely and inaccurately judged the situation — maybe this was the ranger, and she had boarded the windows before actually vacating the area.

"Hello," I offered, standing respectfully at the foot of the small staircase leading up to the porch.

"It's beautiful, isn't it?" she responded and looked around slowly.

"Yeah. I hope it stops snowing by tomorrow though — I need to make it to the top of Whitney," I said as I struggled to match her calm appreciation for the moment.

"Oh marvelous, marvelous," she chuckled.

She seemed sweet but lost in her own world, and the whole scenario made me feel like a fairy-tale protagonist who had just stumbled upon a strange woodland witch.

"Are you a ranger?" I asked, though I was fairly certain what the answer was going to be.

"No, no! I just saw this lonely rocking chair and thought it deserved some company," she laughed.

Locked up for the season after all. I studied the porch, and suddenly a thought occurred to me.

"I was hoping the ranger station would still be open and that I could sleep inside tonight because my sleeping bag isn't warm enough. But since it's closed up, I think I'll just set up my tent right here."

"I don't know that it will help, but I hope it does. I was just about to head back to my tent so I'll leave you to it," she replied, offering her most lucid sentence yet.

I had the macabre thought that it would be anticlimactic and disappointing if I froze to death during the night and this was the last conversation I ever had. At the time I thought nothing of it, but I realize that I often engage in this "worst-case scenario" thinking when under pressure — I think many of us do. At first glance it may seem amusing or even dangerous, but it can be a powerful defense mechanism for warding off anxiety. If I can look my deepest fears in the eyes and find humor in them, they lose some intensity and control over me.

"I ain't afraid of no ghosts"

This exercise may appear to be in direct conflict with my commitment to positivity and visualizing the future that you want to manifest — and if I let it run wild it would overtake me. But in controlled doses it allows me to release tension and create room that I can choose to fill with hope and belief. Like letting yourself have a pity party, I think the efficacy of this activity depends on the energy and awareness behind it.

The now-vacated porch was freshly built and sturdy and consisted of thick-wood planks stacked end-to-end. It was so small that it would barely hold my tent, however it was off the ground and under an overhang. I also hoped the building would provide a wind block. What

I failed to consider at the time was that because it was elevated, cold air could come up between the planks from below. This proved to be a critical error in judgment. (Although I am alive to write this and it is impossible to know how cold I would have been on the ground.)

My tarp-tent is designed to have form and structure while under tension, and since there was no dirt to sink my stakes into I gathered large rocks and used them instead. The platform was not entirely big enough, and the rocks could not create maximum tension, so when I was done setting up my tent it sagged and flapped in the wind like a science experiment gone wrong.

Cold, tired, and frustrated, I threw everything in my tent and climbed in. I would eat and get water in the morning. Right now I just had to get as warm as I could. I was wearing every piece of clothing I owned, and I kept it all on as I wrapped my quilt around me. I lay on my stomach, hands clutching the quilt by my ears, trying to create an airtight vacuum of warmth.

What followed was perhaps the longest night of my life. The bitter chill attacked me like a silent assassin, and my quilt was an ill-equipped bodyguard. I would stay in one spot for a couple tense minutes, and then inevitably I would feel the freeze creep into my quilt and then start on my bones. Eventually sometime in the deepest recesses of the night I managed to find a position on either side that offered slightly more warmth — and by this I mean I was able to stop shivering enough to find brief moments of sleep.

My body temperature dipped dangerously. I had feverish dreams that left me confused and anxious. Both sides of my body represented different gangs, and they were fighting a bloody death match to determine which side got to be warmer. The dreams were vivid, colorful, and frightening, and when I awoke the next morning I felt like I had gone to battle. But I did wake up, and for that I am grateful. I realize now that those dreams kept me moving and engaged, and gave my brain something to do besides obsess about the cold. The mind is truly amazing in its capacity to do what is necessary to overcome.

Chapter 13
Whitney

*(Day 8 – Crabtree Ranger Station to the top
of Mount Whitney, 9 miles)*

*"It is good to have an end to journey toward, but it is
the journey that matters in the end."*
— Ernest Hemingway

I lay on my back for a few minutes watching my smokestack breath rise and dissipate. I noticed that during the night it had woven a tapestry of delicate ice stalactites along the edges of my tarp. Sitting up, I looked through the mesh and discovered that the ranger station had done little to protect me; my tent and I were lone anomalies in a world of white. The sun was slowly coming awake behind a wall of mountains, and the thinly lit sky revealed just enough to put a broad smile on my face. The storm had abated.

As I surrendered to the flowing kata of morning routine, I reflected on my adventure and the simple fact that this would be my last day on the trail. As exhilarating and surreal as that thought was, it also brought a hint of sadness. For someone built like me, the struggle and the journey give life meaning, and I have become addicted to the process of setting audacious goals and then throwing myself at them like a rabid dog. While the climax of achievement is fantastic, the foreplay is where the real growth and enjoyment occurs. This is a common phenomenon in endurance sports, and we actually talk with our athletes about strategies for avoiding depression after completing a big event like Ironman. When all of your energy and force of will is focused on one moment, it is hard not to feel lost when that moment has passed.

Keep your rollercoaster on its tracks

Completing a monumental task (Ironman, thesis, IPO, childbirth, etc.) can carry you to such an incredible vista that afterward you may crash to the rocks below if you're not careful. This scenario can lead to sadness, malaise, boredom, disengagement, and sometimes even clinical depression. Here are my suggestions for healthfully dealing with the doldrums when leading up to a significant life event:

- Acknowledge the need to take these steps in the first place.

- Attempt to step back and really enjoy the process of achieving your goal, rather than just focusing on the end result.

- Look past the completion of the activity and create new goals that excite you.

- Engage with your support network both before and after the event. Talk about these things with the people you love and trust. Avoid isolating yourself.

- Let yourself feel whatever it is you feel. It's okay to be sad. Recognize it, welcome it, and sit with it. Feeling sad doesn't mean you ARE sad — and it doesn't mean you need to "fix" anything. It just means you're human.

My half-full water-bottle had frozen solid overnight, so I stopped at the river to fill up the other one. After quickly treating the water, I thirstily gulped down the entire bottle and then filled it up once more. I had engaged in this exercise countless times along the JMT — would this be the last?

I found the sign pointing toward Whitney, and while the trail was completely covered by snow, there was a lonely set of footprints to guide me. Someone had hiked past during the night or had left before dawn. Either way, I was thankful for the help. I knew the general direction to head, and trails can often be deciphered by paying attention to the contours of the land, but if nothing else the footprints added to the experience, as if the Universe was acknowledging my efforts and welcoming me home.

The terrain would be flat until I began the final climb, and snow flew from my shoes as I moved quickly through it. Now that my summit attempt and life didn't appear to be on the line, I could actually appreciate the winter wonderland I was navigating. It fit well in my survival fantasies, and I couldn't help but feel like kind of a badass.

While currently making my way through a forest, gigantic rock giants loomed up ahead. I wasn't sure which one was Whitney, but with every turn and change of perspective I peered up at them and wondered where I would end this quest. On one occasion when I paused to look up I noticed that tendrils of mist were lazily swirling around the mountaintops that rose thousands of feet above me, and the simple beauty literally took my breath away for a few seconds. Being surprised and thrilled by the perfection of the natural world is one of my favorite things about going on walkabout.

Just minutes later I encountered a flurry of animal tracks in the snow off the trail to my left. I am no tracking expert, but one set of prints had the clawed look of a predator, while the other was smaller and rounder. It looked like there had been a struggle however I didn't see any blood or fur. I grimaced. I was out here trying to cross something off my bucket list and prove something to myself, and some poor rabbit had just become breakfast. Once again, it's all about perspective. I am acutely aware that my issues and demons are insignificant compared to many, and that I am superbly lucky to have had the opportunity to explore them in a manner such as this. Even so, that doesn't diminish the experience for me; after all, we are only ever truly capable of seeing with our own eyes.

I came upon Guitar Lake and was surprised to see just a handful of tents sprinkled around the lake. Most people use Guitar Lake as their final stop before Whitney, and I had read that during the high season it is common for the area to look like a backpacker's bazaar. I noted two people making breakfast and wearing parkas and snow-boots, and realized all the tents at the lake were sturdy four-season beasts that were staked down extensively. It looked like it could be Everest base camp, and yet I was strolling by with trail running shoes, a tarp, a defective quilt, and belief. I shook myself slightly as I considered what a close call last night had been.

And then just like that, I began the last climb of my trip. The trail was covered in re-frozen snow melt, so I had to hop from rock to rock to avoid slipping. A couple times I almost went down and had to use a hand to catch myself, but at no time did I "eat it" completely.

This was the very beginning of the climb, and I still had no real sense of where the trail was taking me as I wound upward. I could see two people a quarter mile ahead of me, and true to my nature I sped up slightly to reel them in. Catching prey is in my genes as a human male, and that drive is exacerbated by testosterone. I have really learned to temper this urge however, because it often doesn't serve me. This was one of my first lessons as I began my

London Bridge is …

I actually didn't fall once during this trip which is incredible considering how many epic tumbles I took during training. Once during a run around Lake Sonoma I was hurtling downhill and tripped over a rock that was lurking under a leaf pile. I was airborne for what felt like minutes, and when I finally struck the ground I rolled two and-a-half times and landed on a rock. I dragged myself back to my car and tried not to let Jen see the dirt and blood on my shirt, because she believes I'm going to kill myself every time I go running, and I hate to offer data that supports that! Anyway, there are two kinds of trail runners (and cyclists for that matter) — those who have fallen and those who will.

transition to endurance athlete. At first I would destroy myself trying to keep people from passing me or attempting to catch someone ahead of me — even during workouts where I was supposed to be taking it easy — and it usually meant I couldn't complete the workout because I was too tired. I would ride farther and faster than my scheduled workout to keep up with friends, and I might skip a recovery day if I was feeling frisky. This is a very common mindset for an amateur endurance athlete, and it can be difficult to overcome. Many never do. But it inevitably leads to injury, fatigue, burnout, and poor performance. And the real learning opportunity has more to do with your mind than your body. Truly, why does it matter what anyone else is doing? Accepting that my journey is my own, and that there is value in it regardless of how it compares to anyone else's has been some of the hardest and most rewarding work of my life. Still, on this day I wanted to catch the quarry in front of me, and I felt like my legs could handle it.

The hikers were in good shape, and I didn't pass them until they stopped to change shoes. They were a young couple who had

been on the JMT for a month and were going to finish today.
I asked them if they were excited to be done, and they both
shrugged noncommittally. They gave the distinct impression of being
somewhere else, as if at some point they had become the trees
and lakes as much as they were themselves. I thought about the
woman in the rocking chair, and the wolf man at Muir Trail Ranch,
and realized I had encountered this before. I suppose losing yourself
is inevitable when you let yourself hear the music of all things. I
wondered if the same process was happening inside me.

I kept climbing higher, and eventually I reached a sign that read
"Mount Whitney Trail — 13,500 feet". This was the last sign before
the top, and indicated that I was two miles and a thousand vertical
feet from the end. Many people leave their packs at this point
because you have to come back down here to get off the mountain,
but I decided to keep mine — it had come 210 miles with me so
it felt right to hold on to it for the last two. This was also the point
where the path from Whitney Portal met the John Muir Trail, and the
rest of the way would be heavy with weekend warriors looking to
conquer Whitney.

The snow and ice became more treacherous. No longer a gradual
gradient, often times I found myself balancing precariously over
rocks hundreds of feet below. Remembering my promise to do
nothing stupid, I slowed down when necessary and paid close
attention to where I put my feet. Even more dangerous were the
questionably qualified day hikers who stopped in the middle of the
narrow trail and often had little awareness of their surroundings.
I quickly learned to give them a wide berth and to announce
my presence before coming upon them. Once I learned how to
navigate around them, they became a source of amusement
because of their stark contrast to the JMT veterans from the other
side of the mountain.

There is a palpable energy exuded by JMT through-hikers, and it's something I've already alluded to. A quiet confidence, a far-away look, the whisper of a knowing half-smile, a certain grit and acceptance of one's place in the world. Their gear is generally fairly Spartan (excluding the techno-pharmacist), their bodies and packs are tight, and there is little wasted movement. The majority of the hikers who had just come up from Whitney Portal couldn't have been more different. Almost all of them were overweight, and the fortune they spent on high-end mountaineering gear did nothing to hide the looks in their eyes: "I am terrified, overmatched, and don't want to be here. I should have prepared better." Even as I judged them, I found compassion. Did I have that look in my eyes the last time I attempted this trail and failed?

I had gradually peeled off the layers of my clothing while climbing, but now that I was exposed at 14,000 feet I realized how cold I felt. As I put my jacket, beanie, and gloves back on I took a moment to look around. The green wilderness I had just traversed stretched to the horizon on my left, the arid plains of Death Valley spread out to my right, and just up ahead was the top of Mount Whitney. The trail jogged to the left and then made a steep right to the top. I couldn't yet make out the exact place I would stop, but I could see the way and feel its closeness.

As I made the turn and entered the home stretch, I was overcome by a feeling of peace. I was proud, immeasurably so, but it was a different satisfaction than I'd felt before. This was a feeling of deep and humble appreciation for what the human spirit is capable of. I felt like I'd touched and channeled something that we all have access to if we're simply willing to open ourselves to it, and that surrender was perhaps the most rewarding part of the journey. We are surrounded and enveloped by so much radiance and power. Why does it scare us so much to embrace that power, to let it thrum with every beat of our hearts, and to fully see and be seen?

Like Muir Pass, there is a hut at the top of Whitney where hikers can take shelter from the elements. Savoring the last steps of my trip, I walked slowly past the hut with barely a glance, eyes focused on the flat rocks ahead. And then my feet could carry me no further. At that moment the highest point in the Continental United States was … me.

I looked down at my watch. It was 10:30 a.m., making my total trail time roughly six days and 18 hours. I narrowed my eyes, clenched my jaw, and nodded to myself. And then I raised my arms and looked to the sky triumphantly like I'd done in my mind a thousand times before. John Muir Trail complete. I finally had my answer.

Chapter 14
Coming Home

(Mt. Whitney to Whitney Portal, 11 miles.
Whitney Portal to Sacramento, 343 miles)

"Not all those who wander are lost."
— J.R.R. Tolkein

I lowered my arms and sat down on the rock. I would eat, record an exuberant video journal entry (that may or may not have contained some inappropriate language), have my picture taken, and sign the registry by the hut — but for a time I just sat and looked out at the world. It was an odd feeling to have achieved my goal but still be far from done.

I took my time, soaking up everything I could, fully aware that I was in the middle of a once-in-a-lifetime experience. I now had less than two hours to travel the 11 miles straight down to Whitney Portal and meet my dad. It would be close, because while most of it would be downhill it was also rocky and treacherous. It wouldn't be a big deal if my dad had to wait for me, however I decided to make a game of it and vowed to beat him to Whitney Portal. I imagined him pulling into the parking lot with excitement, getting out of his car, and looking around expectantly, and then deflating a little as he realized I wasn't there yet. This image motivates me so strongly that I am alive with energy even as I write this — and it definitely supercharged me as I left the top of Whitney.

"You're a good man, Charlie Brown."

My dad and I are close, and there are too many layers and currents that make up our relationship to sort through all of them. But I believe the power in the imagery of him waiting for me stems from a fairly recent experience we had at the Maui marathon. It was my first marathon, and I was brimming with confidence and expectation. My parents came to watch me, and they stationed themselves along the course based on time projections I gave them. I won't bore you with the whole story, but I went out too fast, then went faster up a hill to pass a particularly foul woman (body odor and gas), and then my entire body cramped. It took me such a long time to reach my parents that they started to wonder if they missed me. When my dad saw how much pain I was in he immediately jumped onto the course and finished the race with me, lifting my spirits and keeping me moving. He was wearing Tevas, and they tore his feet to bloody shreds — but he never said a word. I am blessed in that I know my dad is proud of me no matter what I achieve, but I think it makes him happy to see me proud of myself. (The other interesting piece of this story is that because of the open wounds on his feet he contracted a rare and dangerous infection while snorkeling and almost had to have his leg amputated!)

Excited to see my family, overjoyed to have finished what I started, and knowing the rest was downhill — I moved fast. I hop-scotched around day hikers until the Whitney Portal turnoff, and then began descending steep, winding switchbacks. I was grateful for the cool temperature, because this mountainside was fully exposed to the sun. I could foresee what a slog it would be on a hot day.

I ran without slowing or stopping, and yet never seemed to get anywhere. I imagined I was coming down from heaven. I don't know if it was the season or time of day, but on this trail that is often a highway of humanity, I was all but alone; which is why I was startled when I turned a bend and almost ran into a leathery man who was wearing tattered clothing and missing more than a few teeth.

"Sorry, sir," I said as I stepped aside to let him pass.

Then I noticed that his shirt said "Badwater," and I immediately had to question the conclusions I had already made about him. Badwater is a 135-mile running race that stretches from Death Valley to Whitney Portal. Runners have to climb over 8,000 feet and generally face temperatures well over 100 degrees, particularly on the blacktop that covers much of the course. Many people might consider me crazy for attempting to complete the entire John Muir Trail, but I believe there are levels of crazy. Anyone who has done Badwater is insane — however I have intense respect for the amount of mental strength and pain tolerance required. This man may be hanging on by a thread, but it is probably a stronger thread than most people would assume just by looking at him.

"Badwater. Nice," I said, raising my eyebrows with admiration. His eyes focused and looked at me, and his slumped shoulders straightened slightly.

"That's right. This is my backyard," he replied with a jack-o-lantern grin.

We spoke for a few minutes, exchanging ultra-running war stories. He seemed to enjoy finding someone from my generation who could appreciate the miles he'd traveled. As I wished him well and started on my way, he left me with this haunting assertion:

"Beware of long-distance running. She is a mistress that can't be satisfied, and she'll leave you empty and broken if you're not careful."

I thought about these words as I continued my rapid descent, and while I could feel the truth behind them I also felt certain that intent was the key. Why are you running? If, like many endurance athletes, you run to outpace an encroaching darkness, eventually you will be swallowed by it no matter how far you go. I think this is what the old runner was referring to. However if you run because it connects you to something bigger than yourself, or as a moving meditation that allows you to explore your demons rather than flee from them; I have to believe this is restorative rather than destructive.

Downward I flew, until I eventually left the ugly rock behind and began moving through thick forest. Just before entering the shade of the trees I stood at the top of the valley and could see it extend below me for miles. It was strange to have been running downhill for thousands of feet, and yet be standing here at the top of something, still higher than almost everything alive.

I kept looking at my watch, and even with my speed it would be nearly impossible to reach Whitney Portal by 1:00 p.m. But when I saw a sign that indicated I was just four miles away, I shifted into a higher gear that was unknown to me until that moment. Hours in the gym, thousands of miles traveled, the fierce energy created by crashing through a limiting belief, the profound desire to hug my dad and kiss my wife — all of these things gave me the means and fuel to move like I never had before. I know it sounds like storytelling, but I tell you now in all honesty I moved down that mountain in a blur. And the strangest thing is that it was easy. I was pure movement.

Just after 1:00 p.m. I turned the last bend and sprinted into the Whitney Portal parking lot, feet touching pavement for the first time in a week. I stopped moving, and the silence and tingling nerve endings made me momentarily dizzy. I looked around, did a lap through the parking lot, and realized with disappointment that I'd beaten my dad there after all.

I pulled out my cell phone and discovered that if I sat in one corner of the parking lot I could get occasional service. While the signal wasn't strong enough for voice communication, I managed to reach my dad via text and discovered that he was roughly 30-minutes out. (It turns out this was due to a miscommunication that was entirely my fault — otherwise he would have been there waiting as I came off the trail.) I then tried calling Jen, also to no avail, and settled for sending her an exultant text message.

Journey complete and nothing to do but wait, I suddenly realized I was ravenous. I walked up the parking lot to the Whitney Portal Store, and the scent of fried food saturated my senses as I opened the door. Normally this would make my stomach turn, but on this day it fueled the hunger. Without even looking at the menu, I walked up to the counter.

"I'd like a cheeseburger with no bun and a big plate of French fries please," I said with calm conviction.

The woman across from me gave me a knowing smile and nodded.

"Coming right up."

That was the best burger I've ever eaten — maybe the best food I've ever eaten. As I wolfed down my food, I texted with Jen and other friends and family, and truly relaxed for the first time in weeks. The pressure I'd been feeling for so long was gradually letting go. I was done. I had made it.

When my dad pulled into the parking lot I thought I might cry. In fact, while I was on the trail imagining seeing my family I could move myself to the beginnings of tears. However when he got out of the car and gave me a bear hug I felt nothing but joy. I've experienced this at the end of other long-distance endurance events as well. After watching scores of stoic athletes break down at Ironman finish lines I expected that I'd be no different. It makes sense. Months or years of preparation and sacrifice have brought you to one moment — of course you will be charged with strong emotion that bursts free. But I am always too happy to cry.

"Hey, Goobs," he said. Then he smiled, looked me in the eyes, and dipped his head in quiet appreciation for what I'd just accomplished. (Goobers or "Goobs" has been his nickname for me since I was a baby — apparently I looked like a peanut.)

"Hey, dad, "I replied, meeting his eyes and trying to convey a week's worth of experience with a look.

"Let's go home," I said.

As we drove up Highway 395 toward my car and Yosemite, we talked about everything and nothing. Mostly he just let me ramble as I attempted to sort through and integrate everything I had just experienced. I called my mom and had a brief but heartwarming discussion with her — there is nothing that compares to a mother's intense desire to protect when her offspring is in danger, and the release of emotion once that child is safe. While I have to admit this nurturing imperative has felt oppressive at times, it is sublime to feel how much I am loved.

Eventually I was starving again, as if my body was thawing from some great hibernation. We stopped at a grocery store, and as the sliding doors opened I could instantly feel how the trail had changed me. I stared at an enormous mound of red apples just waiting to be eaten. And then I looked past them at the unfathomable multicolored abundance of fruits and vegetables piled high, shining with the promise of sweet nourishment. All this food and nobody had to carry it here on their backs. Amazing.

The other thing that was very apparent as I dazedly wandered through the store was that women were strongly reacting to me. Whether they were positively responding to my stubble and the cologne of the wild or negatively responding because I looked homeless and lost, I can't say. But I felt the weight of their eyes on me, and it was not wholly pleasant. I wondered if zoo animals felt this way. In hindsight they may also have been reacting to the fact that I was completely uninterested in them. I was focused entirely within, and I wanted to see my wife with every fiber of my being. In my experience women are like cats — the less interest you show in them the more they try to rub up against you. Hell, I guess we're all like that.

Back on the road, we made good time and pulled up to my car just as dusk started to slowly capture the sky. When I had left Tuolumne Meadows a week before, the warmth on the breeze and colors reflected by the river spoke of a place still steeped in summer; however last night's snowstorm trumpeted the changing of the seasons and had painted Yosemite in white. I gave my dad another hug, thanked him for giving up his entire Sunday to pick me up, and then got in my car. I was now just one leg away from the end.

As I pulled onto the road I was immediately struck by how uncomfortable it was to be behind the wheel of a vehicle. I hadn't noticed it as a passenger, but now that I was in control the speed felt foreign and dangerous. For a week my feet had been my only source of locomotion, and my reaction time wasn't tuned for driving a car. I was luckily able to rally enough to make it home in one piece, however the amount of concentration and focus required was significant! It would take days before I recalibrated completely.

Full darkness fell, and as we wound through the park I became mesmerized by the taillights of my dad's car in front of me. It occurred to me that in some form or fashion I had been following him my whole life. I had a master's degree, but he had two — plus a PhD. I'd run marathons, but so had he — much faster. I've never felt competitive with him, and he has always supported and encouraged me. But was ultra endurance (and this John Muir Trail adventure) a way to forge my own path and declare my uniqueness and independence? Or was it more about our shared belief that life is meant to be lived? I don't know. But I do know that at some point I stopped to get gas and I watched his taillights dwindle in the distance.

I hadn't yet called Jen because I didn't want to be "schmoopy" in front of my dad, and because it seemed ill-advised to pull out my phone while maneuvering through dark mountain roads that were covered in snow. So I called her as I waited for my car to fill with gas. We spoke briefly about the ordinary but wonderful things that hold us together, and then I got back in my car for the final stretch.

Walking into our house was one of the most powerfully touching moments of my life. The look of love and pride on Jen's face, the joyful dance of our pets, the circle closing — it was indescribable. I reached out to her hesitantly because I hadn't showered in a week ... and because I was changed. When I apologized she said, "I don't care. You're home." I buried myself in her neck, let her scent and warmth fill me to overflowing and realized she was right. I was home.

Appendix

2013 JOHN MUIR TRAIL
PACK LIST

KEY ITEMS

Backpack: OMM Classic Marathon, 32L

Sleeping pad: Thermarest NeoAire X Lite

Water purifier: SteriPen Adventurer

Tent: Z Packs Hexamid Solo Tarp-Tent (with Tyvek ground sheet)

Sleeping quilt: Enlightened Equipment Revelation Slim, 20 degrees
(This is the quilt that nearly led to my frozen demise. I had a good
conversation with the owner of the company and he believes
the Slim size was too narrow for me and the Regular would have
provided more warmth)

Inflatable pillow: ExPed ULM

Personal Locator Device: Spot II

Headlamp: Princeton Tec Remix

Bear canister: Lil Sami Lighter 1 (2nd attempt only)

Sleeping bag liner: Silk Cocoon Mummy Liner (2nd attempt only)

CLOTHING

Waterproof jacket: Outdoor Research Helium 2

Waterproof pants: Nike running pants

Compression tights: Sugoi Piston 200

Gloves: Mizuno Breath Thermo

Beanie: Mizuno Breath Thermo

Shoes: New Balance Minimus Trail 110

Socks: Inov8 Gaitor Socks (2 Pairs)

Hat: Bright orange Adidas baseball hat that has seen many adventures

Vest: Montbell Thermawrap Sport (2nd Attempt only)

T-Shirt: C9 tech tee (Target brand. Yeah, that's how I roll)

Thermal undershirt: Generic

MISC

Platypus Big Zip SL 60 oz water resevoir with hose

Two 24 oz plastic water bottles

Casio Exilim camera

First Aid kit (Homemade and very minimal. Contained Ibuprofen, Band-Aids, and a blister kit)

Sunscreen

Sunglasses

Tom Harrison John Muir Trail Map-Pack

Toilet paper

Body Glide

50 ft of 3mm nylon rope (1st attempt only)

iPhone

Car keys

2013 JOHN MUIR TRAIL
DAILY FOOD LIST

Food	Serving Size	Calories	Fat	Carbs	Protein	Total Weight (g)
Spiz	8 scoops	1034	10	188	40	270
Coconut Oil	2 Tbsp	260	28	0	0	28
Almond Butter	2 packets	360	32	12	14	64
Caveman Bars	2 bars	420	28	30	12	80
Two Moms in the Raw Bars	1 bar	260	18	26	4	56
Rise Bars	2 bars	520	30	44	34	120
Raw Revolution Bars	4 mini bars	400	24	44	12	88
Homemade pemmican	2.5 oz block	500	47	0	19	70
Wild Salmon Packs	1 Pack	240	14	2	25	100
TOTALS (PER DAY)		3994	231	346	160	876
			51%	33%	16%	1.9 LBS

About The Author

Josh Mathe is passionate about squeezing every last drop from life and helping others do the same. He is a speaker, author, fitness expert, nutritionist, ultra endurance athlete, and life adventurer. When he is not speaking at events or running through the wilderness, Josh works with individual clients as the owner of One10 Performance & Nutrition and the Executive Director for the Sustainable Health Institute. Josh holds a Master's of Science in Human Nutrition, and is a certified sports nutritionist (CISSN), Performance Enhancement Specialist (PES), and run coach. He lives in Sacramento, CA with his wife and three crazy animals.

For more information or to contact Josh directly, please visit www.joshmathe.com